CISTERCIAN STUDIES SERIES: NUMBER TWO HUNDRED SIXTY-FOUR

Saint Æthelwold of Winchester

The Old English Rule of Saint Benedict

with Related Old English Texts

CISTERCIAN STUDIES SERIES: NUMBER TWO HUNDRED SIXTY-FOUR

Saint Æthelwold of Winchester

The Old English Rule of Saint Benedict

with Related Old English Texts

Translated and Introduced by
Jacob Riyeff

α

Cistercian Publications
www.cistercianpublications.org

LITURGICAL PRESS
Collegeville, Minnesota
www.litpress.org

A Cistercian Publications title published by Liturgical Press

Cistercian Publications
Editorial Offices
161 Grosvenor Street
Athens, Ohio 45701
www.cistercianpublications.org

Scripture texts in this work are translated by Jacob Riyeff.

Cover art: © The British Library Board, Add. 49598, f 99v.

1   2   3   4   5   6   7   8   9

Library of Congress Cataloging-in-Publication Data

Names: Benedict, Saint, Abbot of Monte Cassino, author. | Aethelwold, Saint, Bishop of Winchester, approximately 908–984. | Riyeff, Jacob, 1982– translator, editor.
Title: The Old English Rule of Saint Benedict : with related Old English texts / Saint Aethelwold of Winchester ; translated and introduced by Jacob Riyeff.
Other titles: Regula. English
Description: Collegeville, Minnesota : Cistercian Publications, 2017. | Series: Cistercian studies ; 264 | Includes bibliographical references and index.
Identifiers: LCCN 2017043542 (print) | LCCN 2017024124 (ebook) | ISBN 9780879072643 (paperback) | ISBN 9780879074982 (ebook)
Subjects: LCSH: Benedictines—Rules. | Monasticism and religious orders—Rules. | Aethelwold, Saint, Bishop of Winchester, approximately 908–984. | Monasticism and religious orders—England—History—Middle Ages, 600–1500. | BISAC: RELIGION / Christianity / Catholic.
Classification: LCC BX3004 .E6 2017b (ebook) | LCC BX3004 (print) | DDC 255/.106—dc23
LC record available at https://lccn.loc.gov/2017043542

For Sr. Pascaline Coff, OSB

Fructus autem iustitiae
in pace seminatur facientibus pacem.
James 3:18

Contents

Abbreviations of Authors and Works Cited

Bede   Bede the Venerable (673–735)

      HE   *The Ecclesiastical History of the English People.* Edited and translated by Bertram Colgrave and R. A. B. Mynors. Oxford: Clarendon Press, 1969.

Blackwell   *Blackwell Encyclopedia of Anglo-Saxon England.* Malden, MA: Blackwell, 1999.

CS   Cistercian Studies Series

CSEL   Corpus scriptorium ecclesiasticorum latinorum. Vienna, 1866– .

Fry   *RB 1980: The Rule of Saint Benedict.* Edited by Timothy Fry. Collegeville, MN: Liturgical Press, 1981.

Gregory   Gregory the Great (540–604)

     Moral   *Moralia in Iob.* Edited by Marcus Adriaen. Corpus Christianorum, Series Latina 143, 143A, 143B. Turnhout: Brepols Publishers, 2005. English translation in *Moral Reflections on the Book of Job.* 6 vols. Translated by Brian Kerns. CS 249, 257, 258, 259, 260, 261. Collegeville, MN: Cistercian Publications 2014–2017. (Vols. 5 and 6 forthcoming.)

   Reg past   *Regula Pastoralis (Pastoral Care). Regola pastorale = Regula pastoralis.* Edited by Giuseppe Cremascoli. Rome: Città nuova, 2008. English translation in *Pastoral Care.* Ancient Christian Writers 2. Translated by Henry Davis. Mahwah, NJ: Paulist Press, 1978.

Gretsch	Mechtild Gretsch
DRB	*Die Regula Sancti Benedicti in England und ihre alteng-lische Übersetzung*. Munich: Wilhelm Fink Verlag, 1973.
IF	*The Intellectual Foundations of the English Benedictine Reform*. Cambridge: Cambridge University Press, 1999.
Reform	"The Benedictine Rule in Old English: A Document of Bishop Æthelwold's Reform Politics." In *Words, Texts, and Manuscripts: Studies in Anglo-Saxon Culture Presented to Helmut Gneuss on the Occasion of his Sixty-Fifth Birthday*. Edited by Michael Korhammer. Cambridge: D. S. Brewer, 1992. 131–58.
Trans	"Æthelwold's Translation of the *Regula Sancti Benedicti* and its Latin Exemplar." *Anglo-Saxon England* 3 (1974): 125–51.

| RB | *RB 1980: The Rule of Saint Benedict*. Edited by Timothy Fry. Collegeville, MN: Liturgical Press, 1981. |
| RB 1980 | Latin text from Fry |

| Schröer | Arnold Schröer, ed. *Die angelsächsischen Prosabearbei-tungen der Benediktinerregel*. 2nd ed. rev. by Helmut Gneuss. Darmstadt: Wissenschaftliche Buchgesell-schaft, 1964. |

Smaragdus	Smaragdus of St. Mihiel (ca. 760–ca. 830)
Comm	*Commentaria in regulam sancti Benedicti; Commentary on the Rule of St. Benedict*. Translated by David Barry. CS 212. Kalamazoo, MI: Cistercian Publications, 2007.
Expositio	*Smaragdi abbatis Expositio in Regulam S. Benedicti*. Edited by K. Hallinger, et al. Corpus consuetudinum monasticarum 8. Sieburg, Germany: F. Schmitt, 1974.

| Vulgate | *Biblia Sacra: Iuxta vulgatem versionem*. Edited by Robert Weber. 2 vols. 3rd ed. Stuttgart: Deutsche Bibelgesellschaft, 1983. |

Whitelock   "An Account of King Edgar's Establishment of Monasteries." In *Councils and Synods with other Documents Relating to the English Church: I, A. D. 871–1204*. Edited by Dorothy Whitelock. Oxford: Clarendon Press, 1981. 142–54.

Monasteries Associated with the Tenth-Century Anglo-Saxon Benedictine Reform

N

Stow

Burton

Peakirk · Crowland · St. Benet at Holme ·
Peterburough · Thorney

Coventry · Ramsey · □ Chatteris
Ely

Worcester · St. Neots · Bury St. Edmunds ·
Pershore ·
Evesham ·

Deerhurst · Winchcombe
Gloucester ·

Eynsham · St. Albans ·
Abingdon ·

Malmesbury · □ Barking
Westminster ·

Westbury ·
Bath · Chertsey ·
□ Bradford

Wherwell St. Augustine's ·
Amesbury □ □ Old Minster Christ Church ·
Athelney · Glastonbury Wilton □ · New Minster
Muchelney · Shaftesbury Romsey
Cranborne · □ Nunnaminster
□ Horton
Cerne · · Milton

Exeter ·
· Abbotsbury

Tavistock ·
Buckfast ·

0   50   100 km

0   50 miles

■ Monasteries of Men
□ Monasteries of Women

Design by Chris Waters, after Sarah Foot, *Monastic Life in Anglo-Saxon England,
c. 600–900*, fig. 1.

Monasteries Founded and Refounded by St. Æthelwold

N

● Crowland
■ Thorney
Peterborough ▲
▲ Ely
■ St. Neots

● St. Albans

▲ Chertsey

▲ Old Minster
▲ New Minster
▲ Nunnaminster

▲ Milton

0   50   100 km
0   50 miles

■ Original foundations of Æthelwold
▲ Refoundations of Æthelwold
● Possible foundations of Æthelwold

Design by Chris Waters, after Sarah Foot, *Monastic Life in Anglo-Saxon England,*
c. 600–900, fig 1.

Introduction

I. A Translation of a Translation?

Old English is the name given to the ancestor of Modern English as it was spoken and written ca. 450–1100 (roughly the "Anglo-Saxon period"). During the latter half of the tenth century, the Latin *Regula Sancti Benedicti* (hereafter, the Rule) was translated into Old English, and this text has come down in five complete manuscripts (including one updating of the Old English into early Middle English) and four additional fragments.[1] It is widely agreed upon by scholars that Saint Æthelwold of Winchester (904x9–984),[2] abbot of Abingdon and bishop of Winchester, is responsible for this Old English translation.[3] While a faithful translation overall, the Old English Rule cannot be described accurately as literal, for it contains a large number of Æthelwold's additions as well as some compressions and omissions of Benedict's Latin text. And yet the Old English Rule has received relatively little study from scholars of either monasticism or Old English literature. Its only edition remains Arnold Schröer's German-language edition (1885; reissued in 1964), and it has never previously

---

[1] Oxford, Corpus Christi College, MS 197 (full Old English text [hereafter, OE]); Cambridge, Corpus Christi College, MS 178 (full OE text); London, British Library, Cotton Tiberius A. iii (fragmentary OE text); London, British Library, Cotton Titus A. iv (full OE text); Wells Cathedral Library, MS 7 (fragmentary OE text); Durham Cathedral Library, B.IV. 24 (full OE text); Gloucester Cathedral Library, MS 35 (fragmentary OE text); London, British Library, Cotton Faustina A. x (full OE text); London, British Library, Cotton Claudius D. iii (full Middle English redaction of OE text). I follow the list of manuscripts on Gretsch, IF, 227.

[2] In such date references, "x" denotes a span of years in which an event could have taken place rather than a range of years over which an event did take place, denoted by a hyphen.

[3] For the attribution to Æthelwold, see Schröer, xiii–xviii, 269–72.

1

been translated. Presumably this state of affairs has arisen because the text is a translation of a well-edited Latin text that is widely available in a number of Modern English translations. However, given the importance of the Old English Rule as the first translation of the Rule into a European vernacular language, exemplifying the strategies used to promote the tenth-century Benedictine Reform in England among religious as well as laity, witnessing to the development and standardization of written English in the early medieval period, and providing a window (however clouded) into the spiritual and pastoral concerns of a central figure in the Anglo-Saxon church and early medieval Benedictine monasticism more generally, the text deserves a wider audience than it has previously enjoyed.[4]

This translation is therefore primarily intended for two distinct, but at times overlapping, audiences. The first comprises monastics and others sympathetic to monastic practice and observance who are not equipped to study the Old English Rule in its original language, given that the comprehension of Old English requires specialized study. Whether these readers are engaged in scholarly work on the monastic tradition or are seeking personal edification, I have attempted to make the present volume accessible to those whose primary concerns are the traditions of monasticism and their religious implications, in keeping with Cistercian Publications' mission. While students of monastic culture who are not specialists in the classical languages Latin, Greek, and Syriac have increasingly found their needs for modern translations met, translations from medieval vernacular languages are still often neglected.[5] Attention to such

---

[4] For brevity's sake, I use the word *England* here to refer to the English kingdom, which varied in its boundaries throughout the period we call "Anglo-Saxon England." However, in Æthelwold's day this kingdom was coalescing into more or less what we now think of as England. For a recent examination of the details of this process, see George Molyneaux, *The Formation of the English Kingdom in the Tenth Century* (Oxford: Oxford University Press, 2015).

[5] Exceptions to this trend of inattention to the Old English vernacular tradition include Benedicta Ward, trans., *Christ Within Me: Prayers and Meditations from the Anglo-Saxon Tradition* (Kalamazoo, MI: Cistercian Publications, 2008); the Dumbarton Oaks Medieval Library series, which includes a number of Old English volumes; and the Classics of Western Spirituality volume *Anglo-Saxon Spirituality: Selected Writings*, trans. Robert Boenig (Mahwah, NJ: Paulist Press, 2001).

work is particularly important in Old English, for, earlier than other European peoples, the Anglo-Saxons employed the vernacular in legal and ecclesiastical matters, producing a large corpus of vernacular homilies, prayers, poetry, chronicles, charters, laws, and translations of philosophical and religious texts. A number of these texts bear directly and indirectly on monastic culture and tradition.

The Old English Rule of course speaks directly to monastic issues as a witness to Æthelwold's enterprising use, as bishop and abbot, of the vernacular to forward his program of reform. The very fact of the Rule's translation and dispersal throughout England in the tenth and eleventh centuries demonstrates the value of the vernacular within the sociocultural milieu of late Anglo-Saxon England for expanding the influence of reformed Benedictine monasticism.[6] However, the text also offers a rare opportunity to see how an early medieval abbot and bishop understood the Rule and how he thought to welcome those without Latin training into its spiritual and disciplinary charism.

Æthelwold had a powerful command of Latin and translated the Rule remarkably accurately. However, he also made a significant number of additions—inserting his own interpretations, clarifications, and emphases throughout (without marking them as such), while also incorporating interpretations and commentary from the ninth-century Carolingian abbot Smaragdus of Saint-Mihiel. Æthelwold's translation, therefore, offers the student of monasticism a reasonably reliable text of the Rule, even as, simultaneously, his additions clarify how this abbot and bishop received and sought to teach it in his own time and place.

The second audience for whom the present volume is intended is students of Old English (both beginning and advanced) in search of a translation that can serve as a bridge into the Old English Rule. Therefore, I have provided a Modern English text that remains faithful enough to the original to facilitate the deciphering of the Old English as well as an apparatus that points to the additions and alterations Æthelwold made to the Rule's Latin text. Whether one's area is manuscript studies, lexicography, cultural studies, history,

---

[6] The importance of the Rule for Anglo-Saxon England as evinced by the Old English Rule and its different versions can be found in Jerome Oetgen, "The Old English Rule of St Benedict," *The American Benedictine Review* 26 (1975): 38–53.

religious studies, or literary studies, this translation is intended to open up the Old English Rule as a text that can now be readily accessed and assimilated in the interest of larger interpretive goals. Surely greater study of the earliest vernacular translation of one of the early medieval period's most important texts, as executed by one of the most prominent figures of the Anglo-Saxon church, will bear fruit if Anglo-Saxonists carefully tend to its details.

These two audiences are of course not mutually exclusive, because, at least in part, uniting them helps to (re)imagine the earliest people, religious institutions, religious practices, and language that we call English.[7] Whether the concern stems from a committed religious perspective that seeks spiritual guidance today from a past religious figure, from a dispassionate scholarly perspective seeking greater historical understanding, or from somewhere between, the Anglo-Saxons and their literature have long been a sounding board for how latter-day Anglophones understand their origins and traditions. Whether this search seeks to return to the sources, to catalogue them disinterestedly, or carefully to avoid repeating their mistakes, understanding of these sources and their contributions to posterity will be fuller the more widely and deeply one delves into them.

II. Æthelwold of Winchester and the English Benedictine Reform

As is true of many medieval figures, a number of details concerning the life of Saint Æthelwold of Winchester remain unknown. Yet a number of extant texts shed light on the major events of his life, his religious and political role in the England of his day, and something of his personality. In addition to the Latin life composed after his death by his disciple Wulfstan of Winchester (fl. 996), Æthelwold is mentioned in a variety of later texts bearing on the history of the kingdom—e.g., *The Anglo-Saxon Chronicle*—and the monastic houses

---

[7] For a recent and thorough review of the ways later thinkers of various stripes have used the idea of Anglo-Saxon England to understand their own pasts, presents, and futures, see John D. Niles, *The Idea of Anglo-Saxon England 1066–1901: Remembering, Forgetting, Deciphering, and Renewing the Past* (Malden, MA: Wiley Blackwell, 2015).

that he founded—e.g., the *Liber Eliensis* from Ely. Additionally, a number of surviving texts in Latin and Old English can be attributed to Æthelwold with greater and lesser certainty.

Regarding Æthelwold's childhood, Wulfstan reports in his *Vita Sancti Ætheluuoldi* only that Æthelwold was born in Winchester to noble parents.[8] On the basis of the date of Æthelwold's ordination to the priesthood (934x39), Michael Lapidge and Michael Winterbottom estimate his birth as occurring in 904x9. Once old enough, the young Æthelwold went to King Æthelstan's (893/4–939) court, where he began his education and pursued a secular career before he was ordained to minor orders and the priesthood by Bishop Ælfheah of Winchester. After his ordination, the king sent Æthelwold to Glastonbury, where he became dean and studied grammar, poetry, and the fathers under the then-abbot Dunstan (d. 988). (Dunstan became another influential proponent of the Benedictine Reform movement championed by Æthelwold.) At some point during his tenure at Glastonbury and during the reign of King Eadred (d. 955), Wulfstan records, Æthelwold desired to go to the continent to learn more of monastic observance, but the king's mother, Eadgifu (d. in or after 966), convinced Eadred to make him stay. This is one of many examples of the royal family's apparently vested (and influential) interest in Æthelwold's career.

Once Eadred had prevented Æthelwold from going abroad, he made Æthelwold abbot of the refounded abbey at Abingdon, ushering in a new phase of Æthelwold's career in the English church. Æthelwold brought monks from Glastonbury, Winchester, and London together in his community, which was enriched by an endowment from the king and gifts from the queen. Though Æthelwold had been prevented from venturing overseas, he apparently set out to create an observant monastic community and even sent one of his monks to Fleury to study the observance of the Rule at a reformed continental monastery.

---

[8] Except where otherwise noted, the account of Æthelwold's life presented here is based on the introduction to and text of Wulfstan of Winchester, *The Life of St. Æthelwold*, edited by Michael Lapidge and Michael Winterbottom (Oxford: Clarendon Press, 1991). The volume contains a full account of Æthelwold's life and milieu. For a collection of essays on various facets of Æthelwold's life, career, and influence, see *Bishop Æthelwold: His Career and Influence*, ed. Barbara Yorke (Woodbridge, Suffolk: Boydell Press, 1988).

The close connection between the king and Æthelwold that had made this experiment possible grew even closer under Eadred's successor, King Edgar (943x44–975, r. 959–975), whom Æthelwold probably served as tutor before his appointment as abbot of Abingdon. In 963, Æthelwold was consecrated bishop of Winchester, and in 964 he replaced the secular canons at the Old Minster (his cathedral church) with Benedictine monks, with the support of King Edgar and a letter of Pope John XII. This was the first monastic cathedral chapter in western Europe, and the precedent set here spread throughout England, affecting ecclesiastical organization there until the Dissolution of the Monasteries under Henry VIII (1491–1547) in 1536–1541. With this expulsion of canons and installation of monks in the cathedral church of Winchester, added to the intimate ties between monastics and Crown as well as the urge to reform monastic customs and liturgy along continental lines, the distinguishing traits of the English Benedictine Reform coalesced.

The Benedictine Reform

While the precise details of the chronology, motivations, and extent of the tenth-century English Benedictine Reform continue to be debated, the general features are basically agreed upon.[9] Saints Æthel-

---

[9] For the standard account of the Benedictine Reform in Anglo-Saxon England, see, e.g., David Knowles, *The Monastic Order in England: A History of its Development from the Times of St. Dunstan to the Fourth Lateran Council, 940–1216*, 2nd ed. (Cambridge: Cambridge University Press, 1963), 31–56; Eric John, "The King and the Monks in the Tenth-Century Reformation," in *Orbis Britanniae and Other Studies* (Leicester: Leicester University Press, 1966), 154–80; and the essays in David Parsons, ed., *Tenth-century Studies: Essays in Commemoration of the Millennium of the Council of Winchester and the "Regularis Concordia"* (London: Phillimore, 1975). For revisionary arguments concerning the Benedictine Reform, see, e.g., Julia Barrow, "The Chronology of the Benedictine 'Reform,'" in *Edgar, King of the English 959–975: New Interpretations*, ed. Donald Scragg (Rochester, NY: Boydell and Brewer, 2008); Julia Barrow, "The Ideology of the Tenth-Century English Benedictine 'Reform," in *Challenging the Boundaries of Medieval History: The Legacy of Timothy Reuter*, ed. Patricia Skinner (Turnholt: Brepols, 2009), 141–54; and Christopher A. Jones, "Ælfric and the Limits of Reform," in *A Companion to Ælfric*, ed. Mary Swan and Hugh Magennis (Leiden: Brill, 2009), 67–108. For an overall assessment of the current view of the Benedictine Reform through the eleventh century, see Tracey-Anne Cooper, *Monk-Bishops and the English Benedic-*

wold, Dunstan, Oswald (d. 992), and their supporters sought to establish strict observance of the Rule (known in England before this time but not universally or exclusively observed in monastic communities) by celibate monks and nuns, to free monastic establishments from secular control and their lands from alienation, and to establish a strenuous liturgical observance.

As with reform movements generally, the Benedictine Reform looked back to what was understood to be a better past. This past was complex. The Reform sought monastic ideals in the apostolic community, in the Roman mission to England in the seventh century spearheaded by Saint Gregory the Great and carried out by Saint Augustine of Canterbury (both monks), and in the first flowering of monasticism in England in the great age of Bede. For pragmatic guidance concerning how to effect reform, however, the three primary figures of the English Benedictine Reform looked to the contemporaneous reforms on the continent, specifically those of Cluny and Gorze. These reforms in turn modeled themselves on the particular past represented by the reforms instituted by Saint Benedict of Aniane in the early ninth century under Charlemagne's son, Louis the Pious.[10] Dunstan had resided at St. Peter's in Ghent (which had adopted the reforms of Gorze) during his exile, while Oswald had made his profession at Fleury (following Oda, his uncle and the archbishop of Canterbury).

In expelling the canons from Winchester cathedral and replacing them with monks in 964, Æthelwold insisted on a new vision of community life in the English church. While groups of canons staffed cathedrals throughout the Western church, Wulfstan described the Winchester canons as living dissolutely, having wives but also abandoning these wives for new ones, and neglecting to say Mass. Thus replacing the canons was in part simply a matter of establishing a certain rigor of discipline in the communal religious bodies of the English church. However, the reformers were addressing another systemic issue at the same time.

---

tine Reform Movement: Reading London, BL, Cotton Tiberius A. iii in its Manuscript Context (Toronto: Pontifical Institute of Medieval Studies, 2015), esp. chap. 2.

[10] For a concise and poignant summary of the Carolingian reforms, the continental reforms based upon them, and these reforms' collective influence on the English Benedictine Reform, see Jones, "Ælfric and the Limits of Reform," 76–78.

While the reformers looked back to an idealized monastic past in England (especially prominent in the anonymous Old English text known as "King Edgar's Establishment of Monasteries," now thought to have been written by Æthelwold himself; see Appendix 3), monasticism in pre-reform England was rarely as rigorous as the reformers imagined. Monasteries were often overseen by lay superiors whose positions and incomes were hereditary, and many of the so-called monks held private property. This was not necessarily aberrant behavior—it appears to have been the norm in pre-reform English monasticism.[11] Despite any misconceptions the reformers had about the past, however, their vision for the future of religious life in England was one in which a rigorous observance of the Rule included the communal holding of property among celibate monks.

But such an overhaul of the tenurial system in England needed royal backing, especially since many religious communities' superiors and members came from powerful, land-owning families. So King Edgar's support was essential to the reformers' program. Especially in "King Edgar's Establishment of Monasteries" (Appendix 3) and the *Regularis Concordia*, the code of observance intended for universal adoption throughout English monasteries, the role of the king and queen is stressed. Removing ecclesiastical lands from secular domination (*saecularium prioratus*) became a means to assure rigorous monastic observance and communal ownership. Yet the only way to achieve such freedom from local secular power in early medieval English society was to place the monasteries under royal power (*dominium*). In return, monks and nuns provided spiritual aid to the royal family and the kingdom through their prayers and through centers of learning and stability. Thus the intimate and reciprocal relationship between the English Crown and monasteries was institutionalized under Æthelwold's direction. It should be noted, however, that while the close connection of the Crown and

---

[11] In this vein, it appears that the Cluniac reform was in part based on the same principle of communalizing an establishment's endowment as a first step. For this particular argument, see John, "The King and the Monks." The following paragraph draws on the same source. For a thorough reassessment of Anglo-Saxon monasticism between the conversion and the tenth-century Reform, which probes the nature of religious communities' links with the secular world, see Sarah Foote, *Monastic Life in Anglo-Saxon England, c. 600–900* (Cambridge: Cambridge University Press, 2009).

ecclesiastical power continued in the next generation of the reform, there was what D. J. V. Fisher has referred to as an "anti-monastic reaction" on the part of secular land owners after King Edgar's death, which led to a certain circumspection among these later writers regarding this union and royal power generally.[12]

Regardless of later developments, with royal support Æthelwold followed up his expulsion of canons at the Old Minster by expelling the canons at Winchester's New Minster in the same year. The exceptional "New Minster Foundation Charter," a lavish and illuminated charter that promoted the reform's monastic and royal ideology and that was probably composed by Æthelwold himself, commemorated the refoundation of New Minster in high style.[13] By the beginning of the 970s, Æthelwold had also refounded abbeys at Milton Abbas, Chertsey, Ely, and Peterborough and founded a new monastery at Thorney. His role in refounding and founding monasteries demonstrates his indefatigable efforts at spreading reformed monastic observance throughout England (see map 2, p. xiii).

In addition to these efforts and others,[14] Æthelwold is also now widely recognized as the primary author of the *Regularis Concordia*, the document intended to regularize monastic observance throughout the English kingdom and drawn up after a synod at Winchester around 973.[15] We do not know how widely the text was adopted, but

[12] D. J. V. Fisher, "The Anti-Monastic Reaction in the Reign of Edward the Martyr," *The Cambridge Historical Journal* 10, no. 3 (1952): 254–70. For more recent studies of how these events affected the second generation of reformers, see, e.g., *Ælfric's Letter to the Monks of Eynsham*, ed. Christopher A. Jones (Cambridge: Cambridge University Press, 2009), 47, 49, as well as Andrew Rabin, "Holy Bodies, Legal Matters: Reaction and Reform in Ælfric's *Eugenia* and the Ely Privilege," *Studies in Philology* 110, no. 2 (2013): 220–65.

[13] The text of the "New Minster Foundation Charter" can be found in Dorothy Whitelock, ed., *Councils and Synods with other Documents Relating to the English Church: I, A.D. 871–1204* (Oxford: Clarendon Press, 1981), 119–33.

[14] The most thorough explorations of the texts possibly attributable to Æthelwold, and so of the intellectual contribution of the Benedictine reform to Anglo-Saxon literate culture more generally, is Gretsch, IF.

[15] For an account of Æthelwold's authorship of the *Regularis Concordia*, see esp. Michael Lapidge, "Æthelwold as Scholar and Teacher," in *Bishop Æthelwold*, 89–117, at 98–100. Reflecting our increasingly nuanced picture of the Benedictine Reform, D. J. Dales has argued for the reevaluation of Dunstan's integral role in the compilation of the *Regularis Concordia* and the cooperative nature of the

we do know that at least Æthelwold's student Ælfric of Eynsham (ca. 950–ca. 1010), a major monastic author in his own right, made an abridged version of the *Regularis Concordia* for his own monks naming Æthelwold as the compiler of the larger work.[16] Regardless of how widely the *Regularis Concordia* was adopted, it demonstrates the central importance of the public and communal celebration of an extended liturgy for the ideal of reformed monastic life, since it draws on a number of continental sources from the documents of the Carolingian reforms of Saint Benedict of Aniane to the contemporary customs at Fleury and Ghent. Æthelwold explicitly reveals in the *prohemium* to the work that advisors from these two continental monasteries advised him.

In addition to its importance for outlining the yearly, weekly, and daily observance of the liturgy in the monastery for the Divine Office and (less so) the Mass, the *Regularis Concordia* also demonstrates the vital and official role the Crown was intended to play in monastic life by calling for repeated prayers for the royal house. In combination with his refounding and founding of monasteries and other important achievements, Æthelwold's plan for the daily liturgical life of England's monks and nuns in the *Regularis Concordia* assured his status as a central creative force behind the Benedictine Reform, a coordinated movement that would persist for decades after its origins in the 960s and 970s.[17]

---

movement more generally ("The Spirit of the *Regularis Concordia* and the Hand of St. Dunstan," in *St. Dunstan: His Life, Times, and Cult*, ed. Nigel Ramsay, Margaret Sparks, and Tim Tatton-Brown [Woodbridge, Suffolk: Boydell Press, 1992], 45–56). However, even here Dales admits that "Because the reform of the monasteries was only a part of Dunstan's work as archbishop . . ., it was perhaps inevitable that much of the detailed collation of materials for the final document of the *Regularis Concordia* was masterminded by Æthelwold who was its draughtsman; these wider considerations also help to explain his leading role as the spearhead of the practical monastic reforms and foundations during Dunstan's primacy" (55).

[16] For this text, see *Ælfric's Letter*.

[17] For an account of the second and third generations of the Benedictine Reform, see Cooper, *Monk-Bishops*. Æthelwold's influence carried over into the reign of King Edgar's successors, (less under) Edward the Martyr (r. 975/978) and (more under) Æthelred (r. 978–1013, 1014–1016), for which, see Molyneux, *Formation*, 190, and, for Æthelwold's involvement in tenth-century politics more generally

After such wide-ranging and assiduous efforts, Æthelwold died on August 1, 984. Yet that was not the end of his presence in the English church. After a reported vision and miraculous healing, his remains were translated from his resting place in the Old Minster crypt to the church's choir on September 10, 996. While his cult never spread widely, he was canonized by his community at Winchester.[18] A number of monasteries and churches in England, primarily those associated with Winchester in some way, commemorated him, and parts of the Mass and office for the feasts of his deposition and his translation are extant.[19] Though not widely venerated as a saint today, Æthelwold is still found in the current *Martyrologium Romanum* under August 1, the day of his deposition: "At Winchester in England, the deposition of Saint Æthelwold, bishop, who composed the *Regularis Concordia* in order to renew monastic discipline, which he had learned from Saint Dunstan."[20]

---

as well, see Barbara Yorke, "Æthelwold and Tenth-Century Politics," in *Bishop Æthelwold*, 63–88. For in-depth studies of what is known of the Divine Office in Anglo-Saxon England, see Richard W. Pfaff, ed., *The Liturgical Books of Anglo-Saxon England* (Kalamazoo, MI: Medieval Institute Publications, 1995); Richard W. Pfaff, *The Liturgy in Medieval England: A History* (Cambridge: Cambridge University Press, 2009); and Jesse D. Billett, *The Divine Office in Anglo-Saxon England 597–c. 1000* (London: Henry Bradshaw Society, 2014).

[18] For an account of Æthelwold's cult and how it developed, see Wulfstan, *Life of St. Æthelwold*, xcix–clxvii. For an account of the anachronistic ways in which later scholars received Wulfstan's *vita*, resulting in an emphasis on Æthelwold's harshness as a teacher and master in twentieth-century scholarship, see Alison Hudson, "From Medieval Saint to Modern *Bête Noire*: The Case of the *Vitae Æthelwoldi*," *Postmedieval* 4 (2013): 284–95. A recent and nuanced study on the role of obedience in agency and the formation of identity in Anglo-Saxon England takes one of these moments of perceived harshness in Wulfstan's vita as its point of departure; see Katherine O'Brien O'Keeffe, *Stealing Obedience: Narratives of Agency and Identity in Later Anglo-Saxon England* (Toronto: University of Toronto Press, 2012).

[19] These are edited and translated in Wulfstan, *Life of St. Æthelwold*, cxiii–cxxxvi.

[20] *Vintoniae in Anglia, depositio sancti Ethelwoldi, episcopi, qui, Regularem Concordiam illam exaravit ad monasticam disciplinam redintegrandam, quam a sancto Dunstano didicerat* (*Martyrologium Romanum: ex decreto sacrosancti oecumenici Concilii Vaticani II instauratum auctoritate Ioannis Pauli PP. II promulgatum*, Editio Typica [Vatican City: Libreria Editrice Vaticana, 2001], *sub die* "1 August").

III. The Old English Translation of the Rule

The Old English Rule has come down in nine manuscripts, five of which contain the entire text.[21] On the basis of documentary, stylistic, and philological evidence, scholars widely accept that Æthelwold is the translator responsible for this work.[22] A passage in the *Liber Eliensis*, a twelfth-century chronicle from Ely based on earlier documents (one of which is extant and the other of which dates to the late tenth century), declares,

> King Edgar and Ælfthryth gave to the holy Æthelwold the estate called Sudbourne (which once belonged to a certain *comes* named Scule) and the chirography pertaining to that estate on the condition that he translate the *Regula S. Benedicti* from Latin into English; which he did. Subsequently, however, the blessed Æthelwold donated the estate in question (together with the chirograph) to Ely.[23]

Many scholars have taken this passage to establish the outer dates for Æthelwold's translation of the Rule, since it appears on the surface that the translation was done after Edgar was married (964x965) and before his death (975). "Edgar's Establishment of Monasteries" suggests a similar range of dates.[24] Serving as an accompanying text

---

[21] See n. 1 above.

[22] For a thorough treatment of the evidence for this attribution, see Gretsch, IF, 226–60.

[23] Translation from Gretsch, IF, 230 n. 10. *Æadgarus rex et Alftreð dederunt sancto Æðelwoldo manerium, quod dicitur Suðburn, et cyrographum quod pertinebat, quod comes, qui dicebatur Scule, dudum possederat, eo pacto ut ille regulam sancti Benedicti in Anglicum idioma de Latino transferret. Qui sic fecit. Deinde vero beatus Æðelwoldus dedit eandem terram sancte Æðeldreðe cum cyrographo eiusdem terre* (E. O. Blake, ed., *Liber Eliensis* [London: Royal Historical Society, 1962]). The *Liber Eliensis* is translated as a whole in Janet Fairweather, trans., *Liber Eliensis: A History of the Isle of Ely from the Seventh Century to the Twelfth* (Woodbridge: Boydell and Brewer, 2005).

[24] Scholars now generally accept Æthelwold as the author of "King Edgar's Establishment of Monasteries" in large part because of Dorothy Whitelock's argument in "The Authorship of the Account of King Edgar's Establishment of the Monasteries," in *Philological Essays: Studies in Old and Middle English Language and Literature in Honour of Herbert Dean Meritt*, ed. James L. Rosier (The Hague:

to the Old English Rule (though only extant in a single copy), this text also mentions Edgar's wife Ælfthryth and likewise does not mention the king's death. However, Mechthild Gretsch has marshaled a wealth of evidence (none of it beyond doubt) that Æthelwold may have translated the Rule much earlier in his career (the 940s or early 950s), circulating it within his monastic communities at Glastonbury and Abingdon, and merely published the work at the request of the king and queen in exchange for the estate at Sudbourne.[25] Regardless of these finer points, it seems certain that Æthelwold translated the Rule sometime in the middle of the tenth century and that this project was supported by the royal family.

We do not know what manuscript(s) of the Rule Æthelwold used as his exemplar, but Gretsch has demonstrated that the Latin text belonged to the *receptus* recension.[26] Since the pioneering work of Ludwig Traube, scholars have recognized that the Rule has come down to us in three recensions: the *purus*, found earliest in St. Gall, Stiftsbibliothek 914, and thought to be most closely based on Benedict's original; the *interpolatus*, found in the oldest surviving manuscript of the Rule, Oxford, Bodleian Library Hatton 48, and exhibiting a high degree of variants *vis-à-vis* the *purus* recension; and the *receptus*, the predominant recension throughout Europe from the ninth to the nineteenth century, formed by mixing the two other recensions in a variety of ways.[27]

In England, as was the case throughout Europe, the *interpolatus* recension was widespread in the seventh and eighth centuries. With Benedict of Aniane's reforms, the *purus* recension was promulgated as the authoritative text of the Rule in Carolingian monasteries, yet we have no evidence that this recension ever reached England during the medieval period. Once the *purus* recension was distributed and copied, however, it was mixed with readings from the *interpolatus*

Mouton, 1970), 125–36. Whitelock's findings are further substantiated in Gretsch, IF, 230–33.

[25] Gretsch, IF, 233–60.

[26] See Gretsch, DRB and Trans.

[27] For a more detailed account of the three recensions of the Rule, see *RB 1980: The Rule of Saint Benedict*, ed. Timothy Fry (Collegeville, MN: Liturgical Press, 1981), 102–11, and Gretsch, IF, 241–51.

recension to form the *receptus* recension, and so these latter manuscripts exhibit a wide variety of readings from the two other recensions as well as original readings. Variants present in Æthelwold's text make clear that his exemplar(s) belonged to this last recension, though no manuscript of the Rule from Anglo-Saxon England matches all the variants found in the Old English Rule.[28]

As with the Rule itself, Æthelwold's "text" as a singular entity is somewhat of a fiction. As a group, the nine extant manuscripts exhibit a number of variations in spelling and word choice readings, and, more significantly, though all but one manuscript contain a text clearly intended for male monks, every manuscript shows signs in its Latin or Old English texts (or both) of deriving from a version intended for nuns.[29] Though some of this evidence comes in the form of erased feminine forms that have been written over, more substantial changes take place in some chapters. Most substantially, two chapters in one copy have been replaced by translations of texts other than the Rule, which I include here as Appendix One and Appendix Two. These chapters clearly address the concerns of female communities. There currently exists no consensus among scholars as to whether there was an original copy that was masculine or feminine in form or whether there were two initial texts produced, or whether Æthelwold or a later adapter inserted the substantial changes. In any case, the evidence seems to point toward an original masculine copy that was later adapted by someone other than Æthelwold.

The intricacies of the arguments concerning the development of the text(s) are beyond the scope of this volume, but it is important for the reader of any text composed before the invention of printing to recognize that the single text presented in a modern edition or translation rarely reflects the manuscript evidence. This generality

---

[28] For a detailed examination of all the variants and their corresponding translations, see Gretsch, DRB, 129–56.

[29] For the most detailed analysis of this issue and its implications, see Rohini Jayatilaka, "The Old English Benedictine Rule: Writing for Women and Men," *Anglo-Saxon England* 32 (2003): 147–87. The material in this paragraph draws on this study. However, see also Julie Smith's recent contribution to the debate, which argues for the late introduction of the feminine version based on a historical examination of audience in " 'I Consider Translation Very Rational': A Vernacular Translation of the Benedictine Rule in the Tenth-Century English Monastic Reforms," *American Benedictine Review* 67, no. 1 (2016): 58–80.

is particularly true in the case of the Old English Rule. Despite the complexity of the manuscript witnesses, in this volume I simply translate Schröer's text, as it is the only edition available, includes a significant number of variant readings from manuscripts other than its base text, and presents the two alternative chapters as appendices.

These textual matters aside, Æthelwold's translation is by and large accurate—it appears that there are only one or two places where he did not understand the Rule's Latin, and even there it may be simply that he wanted to change the text for his own milieu.[30] As may be deduced from the largely straightforward style of the translation's rhetoric, the explanatory and interpretive nature of the numerous additions that Æthelwold inserts into the text, and his own comments in "King Edgar's Establishment of Monasteries," it is evident that he sought to make the Rule more accessible and more readily understandable to a population that had interest in the religious and spiritual matters upon which the Rule sheds light but who lacked the skill (or time?) to comprehend the Rule in Latin. In this, Æthelwold's project is not that far off from the goals of a number of modern translations of patristic, monastic, and other religious works, especially in light of the contemporary monastic, oblate, and allied communities that form significant audiences for such material. With the current age's fall-off in the study of Latin and other dead languages, many members of such communities are aided in their religious pursuits by translated texts—even those with some knowledge of the original languages.

IV. Æthelwold's Old English Style

In general, Æthelwold offers his Old English reader a translation balanced successfully between overly literal calques on the one hand and free translations that depart from the literal sense of the Rule on the other. His is, in the main, a close but idiomatic translation into his native tongue. Two significant exceptions to this trend do exist, however.

---

[30] See Gretsch, Trans, 147 n. 5, and Reform 131–38.

At the end of the Prologue, while Æthelwold never strays wildly from the literal sense of the Rule, he presents a rhetorically embellished passage that—in order to exhibit the stylistic features he marshals—has to depart from the Latin more than is usual.[31] While I allow for a certain complexity in my own translation of this passage, I do not attempt to reproduce Æthelwold's stylistic features. He employs what has been called "rhythmical prose" (a stylistic feature reminiscent of Old English poetic meter used at times by Ælfric and Wulfstan [d. 1023]), paranomasia, alliteration, doublets, parallel phrases, rare words, and neologisms, all to finish the Rule's exhortative Prologue in a rhetorically powerful and memorable way. Compared with this passage, much of the translation is sober and mild. On the other hand, chapters eight through twenty, which lay out the liturgical program of Benedict's monastic community, linger closer to the Latin to the point of being unidiomatic.[32] In particular, here Æthelwold translates Latin ablative absolutes with dative absolutes (e.g., translating RB1980 8.4 "incipiente luce" as Old English *upasprunȝenum dæȝriman* [at the onset of daybreak]). Elsewhere, he generally translates Latin syntax into idiomatic Old English syntax— the more difficult syntactic constructions of the Rule lead Æthelwold into some of his freer translations.

Æthelwold's text represents an intermediate step on the way to a written form of Old English that possessed standardized morphological and phonological forms in a regularized orthography, as well as standardized vocabulary. Scholars have traced this "Standard Old English" and "Winchester Vocabulary"—exceptional for a vernacular language of such early date—to Æthelwold's school in Winchester.[33]

---

[31] Gretsch analyzes this passage more fully in IF, 117–21.

[32] See treatment and sources in Gretsch, Trans, 147–48.

[33] For this process of standardization, see especially Helmut Gneuss, "The Origin of Standard Old English and Æthelwold's School at Winchester," *Anglo-Saxon England* 1 (1972): 63–83; Walter Hofstetter, "Winchester and the Standardization of Old English Vocabulary," *Anglo-Saxon England* 17 (1988): 139–68; and Mechthild Gretsch, "Winchester Vocabulary and Standard Old English: The Vernacular in Late Anglo-Saxon England," *Bulletin of the John Rylands Library* 83, no. 1 (2001): 41–87. For an in-depth study of how the language used in the Old English Rule fits into the development of this standardization and the Benedictine Reform culture more generally, see Gretsch, IF.

Most of the additions Æthelwold makes are for the sake of clarity. Doublets (translating one Latin word with two Old English words) regularly occur throughout the work. While some Old English texts translated from Latin appear to present doublets from a sense that one Old English word will not convey the full sense of the original, Gretsch suggests that Æthelwold employs doublets for more nuanced reasons: to convey a variety of semantic components of the Latin word, to convey both a literal and a metaphorical translation, to present synonyms—a practice pleasing enough for its own sake to the medieval mind—and, as a result of the preceding reasons, to achieve greater clarity of expression.[34] These factors, coupled with a frequent use of alliteration (another salient feature of Old English poetics) and other common rhetorical features like paranomasia, suggest that Æthelwold wanted a vigorous, intellectually and aurally exciting text that would assist its readers and auditors to engage with and come to a fuller understanding of the Rule. Unfortunately, many of these features are not reproducible in an idiomatic translation into Modern English, though I have tried to retain or echo them where possible.

What does come through clearly in a Modern English translation is Æthelwold's subtle yet persistent embellishment of the Rule. While the Rule was and is by its very nature a pragmatic and prescriptive text, it is also a central text of the Western spiritual tradition. In the numerous unannounced additions to the Rule's text Æthelwold reveals what appear to be elements of his own spiritual formation and offers guidance on how to understand the Rule's content. He did not set out to write a full commentary on the Rule; by his time, this task had already been accomplished by Smaragdus of Saint-Mihiel and another ninth-century Carolingian ecclesiast, Hincmar of Reims. While it remains unclear whether or not Hincmar's commentary was known in Anglo-Saxon England, Æthelwold certainly knew Smaragdus's commentary and used it to guide his own interpretation throughout his translation.

Æthelwold clearly sought not to expound the intricacies of the Rule for other learned monks and nuns; rather, as he explicitly states in "King Edgar's Establishment of Monasteries," he sought to make

---

[34] Gretsch, IF, 44–45, 113–15.

the Rule accessible to pious lay men and women as well as to new monastics who had not yet learned Latin so that they might have no excuse to plead ignorance of the Rule's stipulations. Another learned commentary was unlikely to accomplish these goals. However, a guided translation or—what Janet Bately has called with respect to the Old English translations of King Alfred's (848x49–899) circle—a "transformation" that leads the reader to more precise understandings of Benedict's text without the intrusion of self-conscious apparatus serves this purpose well.[35]

A good number of the additions found in Æthelwold's translation are straightforward embellishments that apparently seek to make sure that the Rule's meaning is clear. For example, the Latin text of Prol. 39 reads,[36]

> Cum ergo interrogassemus Dominum, fratres, de habitatore tabernaculi eius, audivimus habitandi praeceptum, sed si compleamus habitatoris officium.

> (Brothers, now that we have asked the Lord who will dwell in his tent, we have heard the instruction for dwelling in it, but only if we fulfill the obligations of those who live there.)

While Æthelwold translates the literal sense of the first independent clause with only slight changes, he also spells out for his audience more precisely what he thinks Benedict means by altering the dependent clause following *sed* and expanding it:[37]

> Þa we eornestlice urne drihten ahsedon be þæm buȝendum his eardunȝstowe, we ȝehyrdan hwæt þa ȝebodu synd, þe we þa eardunȝe mid ȝeearnian sceolon; mid ȝefyllednesse ȝoddere þenunge <we weorðaþ heofena rices yrfeweardes>.[38]

---

[35] See Janet Bately, *The Literary Prose of King Alfred's Reign: Translation or Transformation?* (London: University of London King's College, 1980).

[36] The English and Latin quotations of the Rule that follow are from Fry unless otherwise noted.

[37] The quotations of the Old English Rule that follow are from Schröer, while the translations are my own.

[38] Angle brackets indicate Æthelwold's additions in the text of the Old English Rule.

(Now that we have asked our Lord who may dwell in his tent,
we have heard his precepts for meriting this. If we fulfill that
service well, <we will become heirs of the Kingdom of heaven>.)

While the general sense of the verse does not change, it is certainly
different in its particulars—Æthelwold has made explicit what this
verse of Benedict's text only implied: that the *tabernaculum* or *tent* is
the Kingdom of heaven.

In the instance just cited, Æthelwold appears to be inserting his
own reflections and suggestions for understanding into his translation. Yet he makes similar explanatory insertions when he borrows
from prior authorities. For instance, without mentioning either
Smaragdus or Gregory the Great, Æthelwold provides his audience
with an explanation of the scriptural metaphor "to gird our loins"
("Succintis . . . lumbis nostris"). This metaphor is employed in Prol.
21:

> Succintis ergo fide vel observantia bonorum actuum lumbis
> nostris, per ducatum evangelii pergamus itinera eius . . .

> (With our loins girt in faith and the performance of good works,
> let us set out on this way, with the Gospel for our guide . . .)[39]

While Æthelwold also replaces the phrase "with the Gospel for our
guide" with the phrase "with the haven of holy virtues," more important is his interpretation of the metaphor "With our loins girt" as
"with purity of mind and body":

> We eornestlice mid <clænnesse modes and lichoman> and mid
> ȝeleafan and ȝodra weorca biȝȝenȝe and mid <haliȝra mæȝena
> hæfene> his weȝas ȝeornlice faren . . .

> (Therefore, we ought to eagerly tread his paths with <purity of
> mind and body>, faith and the observance of good works, <and
> the haven of holy virtues>.)

---

[39] "With our loins girt in": my translation to demonstrate the Latin's meaning
more literally; the rest of the translation comes from *RB 1980*.

As above, Æthelwold seeks to make the text's meaning more transparent, but unlike in the previous example, he does not add a phrase but replaces one. Either way, "with purity of mind and body" is not Æthelwold's own contribution to the exegesis of what this scriptural metaphor entails. The meaning he provides is mediated to him twice: more immediately through Smaragdus's commentary and, more remotely, through Gregory the Great's *Moralia in Iob*. Smaragdus comments on Prol. 21 with a quotation from Gregory:[40]

> "Lumbos vero viriliter accingere est, vel in opera vel in cogitatione carnis et mentis luxoriam refrenare."
>
> ("Now to gird one's loins manfully is to curb the impurity of the flesh and of the mind, whether in deed or in thought.")

While Æthelwold's addition is not a direct translation, such similarities to Smaragdus's commentary in thought and phrasing occur too frequently to be reasonably considered coincidental. Yet again Æthelwold, without signaling to his audience that he is altering the Rule's text, transforms the received text in order to elucidate it for an audience he expects to lack the knowledge that he possesses.

Beyond these distinct but relatively straightforward additions to the text of the Rule that make elements left implied in the original explicit, in other places Æthelwold expands on points in ways that do not appear to be interpreting them so much as emphasizing them. In smaller matters, examples such as the following from *RB 1980* 43.3 appear numerous times:

> Ergo nihil operi Dei praeponatur.
>
> (Indeed, nothing is to be preferred to the Work of God.)
>
> Ne sy nan ðinȝ ȝeset toforam þam ȝodes weorce, <ne nan ðinȝ swa besorh, þæt he his tidsanȝ fore forlæte>.
>
> (Nothing is to be preferred to the Work of God, <nothing so loved that he would neglect his canonical hour>.)

---

[40] The Latin quotation here is from Smaragdus, Expositio, while the translation is from Smaragdus, Comm.

Many minor—yet, in their way, arresting—additions like this appear, but at several points it seems as though Æthelwold's concerns as a reformer of monastic life shine through in more substantial additions. One such instance occurs at *RB 1980* 64.1, which prescribes the method of choosing an abbot. Æthelwold expands the verse and shifts the syntax in several ways, but in one early clause and the final clause, he again (as in Prol. 39 above) contributes additions (set off in angle brackets), not expansions:

> In abbatis ordinatione illa semper consideretur ratio ut hic constituatur quem sive omnis concors congregatio secundum timorem Dei, sive etiam pars quamvis parva congregationis saniore consilio elegerit.

> (In choosing an abbot, the guiding principle should always be that the man placed in office be the one selected either by the whole community acting unanimously in the fear of God, or by some part of the community, no matter how small, which possesses sounder judgment.)

> On abbodes hadunȝe a is þæt to besceawiȝenne <mid miclum ȝesceade>, þæt se sy to abbode ȝeset, þe eal ȝeferræden anmodum ȝeþeahte and halwendum æfter ȝodes eȝe ȝecyst; ȝif ȝeferræden þæne ræd on ȝemænum ȝeþeahte misredað and feawa witena þæs ȝeferes þa þearfe forȝode wislicor tocnawað, stande þara ræd, þe mid ȝodes eȝe and wisdome þa þearfe geceosað, þeah heora feawa siȝ. <Ne ða oþre onȝean þæt nan ðincȝ wiðcweðon.>

> (In electing an abbot, the aim—<taken up with the greatest discretion>—should always be to install an abbot who is chosen by the entire community in unanimity and wholeness in accord with the fear of God. If in general council the community provides bad counsel and a few experienced individuals in the community who possess more wisdom recognize what is necessary, their counsel should prevail, since they make their decision with the fear of God and wisdom though they are few. <The others should offer no resistance to the decision.>)

Æthelwold's reshaping of the section from *sive* to *elegerit* emphasizes the importance of a smaller group with greater wisdom choosing the abbot, but this does not add anything genuinely new to the literal sense of Benedict's text. Yet the warnings that the election "should be taken up with the greatest discretion" and that "The others should offer no resistance to the decision" appear to reflect a certain degree of anxiety about the ability of entire communities reliably and peacefully to choose the correct superior—a concern that would not be out of place in an era of reform that, according to one of its primary architects, needed assistance in understanding the very text that the reform was based upon.

Beyond these additions that seek to clarify ideas left implicit in the Rule, to unpack obscure metaphors, and to regulate monastic communities in the specific historical community of Anglo-Saxon England (examples of all these could be multiplied), perhaps one of the most touching aspects of Æthelwold's translation is the Christological emphasis that this bishop and abbot imports into his text. Whatever we might think of the political and social ambitions he possessed and of his tactics for reforming houses and establishing monastic life through the backing of royal power, we do find notes of a sincere and focused devotion to Christ in Æthelwold's translation, in keeping with *RB 1980* 4.21 ("set nothing before the love of Christ"—"nan þinȝ beforan Cristes lufe settan," as Æthelwold renders it).

Evidence of this Christological focus comes in the rhetorically charged ending to the Prologue mentioned above. Ensuring that his audience understand the final goal and purpose of the Rule, Æthelwold inserts Christ explicitly into two verses in the final paragraph, Prol. 46 and Prol. 48:

In qua institutione nihil asperum, nihil grave, nos constituros speramus . . .

(In drawing up its regulations, we hope to set down nothing harsh, nothing burdensome.)

Þeah hwet teartlices hwæthwara stiðlice on þisum reȝule, þe ures færyldes latteow to Criste is, ȝeset and ȝetæht sy . . .

(Though there are some things set out in this rule, <which is a guide on our journey to Christ>, that are a little severe and taught strenuously . . .)

non ilico pavore perterritus refugias viam salutis quae non est
nisi angusto initio incipienda.

(Do not be daunted immediately by fear and run away from the
road that leads to salvation. It is bound to be narrow at the
outset.)

ne beo þu þurh þi forht and afæred, ne þurh yrhþe ðinre hæle
weȝ ne forlæt; þæs weȝes onȝin, <þe to Criste læt>, ne meȝ beon
beȝunnen on fruman butan sumre ancsumnysse . . .

(Nor should you abandon the path of your salvation on account
of sloth. The beginning of this path, <which leads to Christ>,
cannot be begun without some distress at its outset.)

With similar reserve, but in a more substantial way, Æthelwold
also explains Benedict's exhortation to "dash" one's wrongful
thoughts against Christ in *RB 1980* 4.50 (which, though one might
guess as much as Æthelwold offers, could probably use some
explaining):

Cogitationes malas cordi suo advenientes mox ad Christum
allidere et seniori spiritali patefacere.

(As soon as wrongful thoughts come into your heart, dash them
against Christ and disclose them to your spiritual father.)

þa yflan ȝeþohtas, þe him on mod becumað, he sceal sona on
Criste toslean and his ȝastlican lareowe andedtan. <Ðonne he
hie toslyhð on Criste, þonne he ȝeðenceð Cristes þrowunge and
his wundra and mid þæm ȝeþohtum aflymeð þa yfelam
ȝeþohtas.>

(When evil thoughts come into his mind, he must immediately
dash them against Christ and confess them to his spiritual master. <To dash them against Christ, he remembers Christ's passion
and his miracles—with those thoughts he puts the evil ones to
flight.>)

In this short but wise interpretation of Benedict's counsel, we have
a rare and precious example of an early medieval bishop and abbot's
practical suggestion to new monks and layfolk alike as to how one
should ward off temptation. While one might wish that Æthelwold

had inserted more additions like this into his translation of the Rule, any such snatches of the thought processes of and spiritual guidance offered by a learned religious in his own language and in such a remote period are rare gifts to posterity indeed. Such moments prevent Æthelwold's text from being merely a piece of valuable but arcane historical and linguistic trivia and secure it a place as a substantial contribution to the Benedictine tradition.

V. Principles of this Translation

Because Æthelwold's text is an early medieval vernacular translation of an earlier medieval Latin text with which readers will probably be far more familiar, I have approached this translation with the underlying assumption that many readers will use this text as a way of mediating between the Latin and the Old English texts. If one wishes to compare Æthelwold's text to Benedict's Latin text, a freely idiomatic translation may obscure more than it illuminates, and so I have rendered my Modern English closer to a literal translation of Æthelwold's Old English than I otherwise would have. While this approach makes for some admittedly clunky phrasing at times, it is my opinion that ease of comparing this work to Benedict's Latin outweighs a less literal text that would be easier to read on its own but would hinder readers' ability to see clearly how Æthelwold has shaped and transformed his source text. I hope that readers of this book will excuse this strategy, since such texts are not easy reading to begin with. With that said, I have tried to avoid archaism and obviously contorted syntax, and I have broken up many of Æthelwold's longer sentences to facilitate comprehension.

To aid in the effort of understanding how Æthelwold has transformed Benedict's text, I have placed angle brackets within the text to indicate Æthelwold's additions to the Latin text; footnotes throughout keep the reader apprised of his subtractions, replacements, and free translations. Except for doublets, when Æthelwold changes a text substantially I quote the relevant text from the Rule in Modern English translation and Latin from *RB 1980*, unless I note otherwise. I only insert my own translations of *RB 1980*'s Latin if Fry's translation departs from the literal sense to the extent that his idiomatic translation obscures the literal text. I also follow the paragraph division found in *RB 1980* to facilitate comparison of the two texts.

However, although I use *RB 1980,* since it is now a standard text of the Rule in the English-speaking world, I have also noted where Æthelwold clearly translates a variant reading that is not included in *RB 1980.* Fry uses a Latin text based on that established by Jean Neufville and found in the edition by Adalbert de Vogüé, which in turn is based on the *purus* recension (see Fry, 155). Since Æthelwold used a *receptus* text for his exemplar(s), a number of readings throughout his translation do not match the text found in *RB 1980* and yet are clearly faithful translations of his *receptus* exemplar(s) of the Rule. These variants are particularly important for students of Old English and Anglo-Saxon culture. But for all readers of this text and others that have come down from manuscript culture, they are also important witnesses to the variability of pre-print texts. Although editors can take textual variability as evidence of corruption of an original text, in this volume I intend no such judgment on the purity of Æthelwold's text or his exemplar; I simply assume that he had access to certain readings and not others. Finally, although I also note places where it seems that Æthelwold has drawn on Smaragdus for his interpretation, I do not generally indicate Benedict's own dependence on other texts for the Rule; Fry provides citations for these texts in his notes.

In spending the last several years with Æthelwold's Old English text, I have developed a fondness for this relatively obscure ecclesiast from over a millennium ago; I suppose such attachment is common among translators who enjoy their subjects. It is my hope that enough of what I now see in him and his work comes through in these pages that the reader too will find a ready interest in the cultural and intellectual implications of his work but also in his elusive but careful voice, present throughout what follows.

Acknowledgments

It is my great delight to acknowledge several groups of people who have helped this project come to realization in various ways. First, my thanks and filial appreciation go to Sr. Pascaline Coff, OSB, and the Sisters of Perpetual Adoration, especially those who served at Osage Monastery (now Deanery) and first invited me into the Benedictine world. My sincere appreciation also goes to everyone who has taught me Old English over the last decade and more of my life: Drs. Sherry Reames, Dick Ringler, and John D. Niles of the University of Wisconsin at Madison and Drs. Thomas N. Hall and Chris Abram of the University of Notre Dame—thank you all for helping me to develop the skills to do work like this! I also owe thanks to my friends Drs. Andrew Klein, Karl Persson, and Emily Ransom, who let me talk through this project (and so much else) in various ways with them. The practical work of this translation would not have been possible without the assistance of the supportive and generous librarians at the Hesburgh Library at Notre Dame (especially Susan Feirick, Kristie Clark, and Abby Vande Walle), Notre Dame's Medieval Institute (especially Julia Schneider), Raynor Memorial Libraries at Marquette University, and the British Library Board for providing the cover photograph, from MS. Add. 49598, f.99v. My deep gratitude goes to Marsha Dutton, the editor who gave this project a chance and saw it through to print with patience, kindness, candor, and a sustaining sense of humor. And finally and most especially, it is my great honor to thank my parents, David and Kim, for relentlessly encouraging me to read and to learn; my brother, Paul, who pointed out that I should probably finally go to college; my wife, Mamie, who has enthusiastically supported me and my pursuits no matter where they've led us; and my three children, Clara, Selevan, and Abram—*þæt is yrfe eac ecean Drihtnes / and herde bearn, þa her mannum beoð / of innaðe ærest cende* (Ps 126 [127]:3).

The Rule of Saint Benedict as Translated by Saint Æthelwold of Winchester

Here Begins the Prologue of the Rule for Monks.

¹My child, hear the precepts of your master and incline to them with the ear of your heart. Willingly receive your honorable father's admonition and fulfill it boldly, ²that through the labor of your obedience you may turn back to God, from whom you previously turned away in the idleness of your disobedience. ³My discourse and teaching are sent earnestly to everyone who denies his own desires and wishes to obey the true King,[1] Christ the Lord, with the strongest and most excellent weapons of obedience.

---

[1] "own desires": translating the *receptus* reading "propriis voluptatibus" ("own desires") instead of *RB 1980* Prol. 3, "propriis voluntatibus" ("own will") (here and below, when referring to Latin text, *RB 1980* indicates the Latin reading found in *RB 1980: The Rule of Saint Benedict*, ed. Timothy Fry [Collegeville, MN: Liturgical Press, 1981] [hereafter Fry], in order to differentiate this particular text from all the various readings found throughout the many manuscripts of RB, since some readings in *RB 1980* would have been found in Æthelwold's text(s) of the Rule and some would not; see Introduction, 24–25). "wishes to obey the true King": Æthelwold shifts the metaphorical martial imagery of *RB 1980* Prol. 3 ("to do battle for the true King, Christ the Lord") to the literal concept of "obedience," though by Benedict's day Lat *militia* and *militare* also have connotations of "service" more generally, for which see Fry, 158 n. to Prol. 3.

⁴First, as often as you begin a good work, eagerly desire with constant prayer that the Lord may permit it to come to a perfect conclusion. ⁵In this way, our heavenly Father, who considers us his own children, will never be offended by our evil deeds or become wrathful with us. ⁶At every moment, with those good gifts that he has granted us, we ought to obey him, lest he disinherit us—<that is, remove us from his happiness>.² A father disinherits his son <and refuses to grant him his wealth when the latter's sins anger him. Just so, he will not grant us our inheritance, separating us from his wealth>. ⁷Rather, like a fearful lord angered by our evil deeds, he will refuse to grant us his wealth as an eternal punishment if we refuse to follow him to glory.

⁸Therefore, let us now rise up on account of the admonition in Holy Scripture that says, *Now is the time for us to arise from sleep**—<that is, that we leave off our sins and be vigilant in good works>.³ ⁹With the manifest care of heavenly understanding, we should also listen to what the voice from heaven daily reminds us and calls out to us, saying,⁴ ¹⁰*If today you hear God's voice, do not delay nor wish to harden your hearts.** ¹¹Again

*Rom 13:11

*Ps 94 [95]:8

---

² "that . . . happiness": Æthelwold's additions to the Rule (of whatever kind) will be set off by angle brackets throughout the present text.

³ "that . . . works": it is quite possible that Æthelwold has borrowed this interpretation of Rom 13:11 from Smaragdus, Expositio Prol. 8 (24; Comm 73): "Dormit anima, quae commissa praeterita non emendat et de futuris nihil cogitat; vigilat, quae praeterita peccata plangit et plangenda ulterius non committit" ("The soul that does not amend its past sins and has not thought for the future is asleep; the soul that laments its past sins and commits no more that it needs to lament is keeping watch").

⁴ "we . . . what": replacing *RB 1980* Prol. 9, "et apertis oculis nostris ad deificum lumen" ("Let us open our eyes to the light that comes from God").

it says,[5] *He who has ears for hearing, let him hear what the Holy Spirit says to all those who are called to God:*[6]* [12]*Come, my children and hear me; I will teach you the fear of God.* [13]*Run and hasten while you have the light of life, lest the darkness of death seize you.**

*Rev 2:7

*Ps 33 [34]:12

*John 12:35

[14]The Lord seeks and searches in the great multitude of people for those few who wish to do his will. Thus he asks, saying, [15]*Who desires life and wishes to see good days?** [16]If you hear this and answer, "I desire this," almighty God says to you, [17]If you wish to have true and eternal life, *restrain your tongue from evil speech and do not let your lips speak anything deceitful; turn from evil and do good; seek after peace and follow after it.** [18]When you do this, my *countenance will be over* you *and* my *hearing* will attend to your *prayers,*[7]* and *before you call to me, I will say, Even now I am completely at your need.*[8]*

*Ps 33 [34]:13

*Ps 33 [34]:14-15

*Ps 33 [34]:16

*Isa 58:9

---

[5] "and again it says": translating the *receptus* and *interpolatus* reading "et iterum dicit" instead of *RB 1980* Prol. 11, "et iterum" ("And again").

[6] "*He . . . God*": translating *RB 1980* Prol. 11, "*Qui habet aures audiendi quid spiritus dicat ecclesiis*" ("*You that have ears to hear, listen to what the Spirit says to the churches*"). When Æthelwold deviates substantially from the Latin of *RB 1980*'s quotations of the Bible, I follow his translation closely and note the Latin and Modern English from *RB 1980* to illustrate how he conveys biblical material to his vernacular audience. Here he makes explicit what Lat *ecclesiis* means by describing the church, even though OE *circe* would translate *ecclesia* directly, and he uses this word to translate *ecclesia* in 13.10 below. For a discussion of this choice within the larger context of the texts produced in Æthelwold's circle, see Gretsch, IF, 104–13.

[7] "my *countenance . . . prayers*": translating *RB 1980* Prol. 18, "*oculi* mei *super* vos *et aures* meas ad *preces* vestras" ("my *eyes will be upon* you *and* my *ears will listen for* your *prayers*"). "my countenance": Æthelwold may have translated Lat *oculi* ("eyes") as OE *ansyn* ("countenance") with an eye toward Ps 33 [34]:17, which refers to God's *vultus* ("face" or "countenance").

[8] "and . . . need": translating RB Prol. 18, "*et antequam me invocetis dicam* vobis: *Ecce adsum*" ("*and even before you ask me, I will say to you: Here I am*").

¹⁹What is more desirable to hear than this voice of God calling out to us? ²⁰Even now, in his mercy the Lord shows us the paths of life. ²¹Therefore, we ought to eagerly tread his paths with <purity of mind and body>,⁹ faith and the observance of good works, <and the haven of holy virtues>. Thus we may merit to see

*1 Thess 2:12   the one *who called* us <to that path> *in his kingdom.**

²²And yet the tent of his kingdom is reached only with care and the observance of good deeds;¹⁰ <zeal and diligence in good works form the course of the path leading to that kingdom>. ²³But let us ask our Lord in accord with the prophet's admonition, saying, *Lord, who may dwell in your tent, and to whom is rest upon*

*Ps 14 [15]:1   *your holy mountain granted?** ²⁴After this question we must listen to the Lord, who answers and who shows us the path to his tent: ²⁵*He who remains without the contamination of sins and walks in just works goes on the correct path to my kingdom,* ²⁶*who considers the truth in his heart and speaks no deceitful thing with his mouth,* ²⁷*who does no evil to his neighbor, who does not set reproach*

---

⁹ "with purity of heart and body": it appears that Æthelwold transfers the metaphorical Lat phrase *"succinctis . . . lumbis nostris"* (*"with our loins girt"* [my translation]) to the more literal "purity of heart and body" to make clear the appropriate preparation for the monastic life. It is possible that Æthelwold has taken his cue in this refashioning of *RB 1980* Prol. 21 from Smaragdus, Expositio Prol. 21 (35; Comm 89), which draws on Gregory's twofold interpretation of the scriptural phrase "to gird one's loins": "Lumbos vero viriliter accingere est, vel in opera vel in cogitatione carnis et mentis luxoriam refrenare" ("Now to gird one's loins manfully is to curb the impurity of the flesh and of the mind, whether in deed or in thought") (see Gregory, Moral 28.III.12; CCSL 143B:1402).

¹⁰ "And . . . deeds": translating *RB 1980* Prol. 22, "In cuius regni tabernaculo si volumus habitare, nisi illuc bonis actibus curritur, minime pervenitur" ("If we wish to dwell in the tent of this kingdom, we will never arrive unless we run there by doing good deeds").

and scorn upon his neighbor,[11]* [28]who rejects the cursed
devil from his heart, that teacher of every evil, along
with all his teaching, taking no account of him, and
who places all his thoughts and hopes in God.[12]* [29]And
those who fear God and do not exalt in their good
deeds.[13]* [30]Rather, *these praise* and celebrate the Lord
who works the good in them,* saying with the
prophet, *Not to us, Lord, not to us, but to your name be
the glory.*[31]Similarly, Paul took no praise for his great
preaching <but gave all the praise to God, who had
given him prudence and wisdom>, saying, *Through
God's grace I am what I am.*[32]Again Paul says concerning himself, *He who glories should glory in almighty God
and not in himself.*[14]* [33]Concerning this same notion the
Savior says in the holy gospel, calling out, *I liken the
one who hears these words of mine and fulfills them in his
works to a wise man who built upon solid stone.* [34]*Floods*

*Ps 14 [15]:2-3

*Ps 14 [15]:4;
Ps 136 [137]:9

*Ps 14 [15]:4

*Ps 14 [15]:4

*Ps 113 [115:1]:9

*1 Cor 15:10

*2 Cor 10:17

---

[11] *"He . . . upon his neighbor"*: translating *RB 1980* Prol. 25-27,
"dicens: *Qui ingreditur sine macula et operatur iustitiam; qui loqui-
tur veritatem in corde suo, qui non egit dolum in lingua sua; qui non
fecit proximo suo malum, qui opprobrium non accepit adversus
proximum suum"* (*"One who walks without blemish, he says, and
is just in all his dealings; who speaks the truth from his heart and has
not practiced deceit with his tongue; who has not wronged a fellowman
[sic] in any way, nor listened to slanders against his neighbor"*).

[12] *"and . . . God"*: replacing *RB 1980* Prol. 28, "respuens,
deduxit ad nihilum, et parvulos cogitatos eius *tenuit et allisit ad
Christum"* ("While these temptations were still *young, he caught
hold of them and dashed them against* Christ").

[13] *"who fear God"*: translating *RB 1980* Prol. 29, *"timentes
Dominum"* (*"those who fear the Lord"*). Æthelwold frequently
translates titles for the deity interchangeably; e.g., here he uses
"God" (Lat *deus*; OE *god*) where the literal translation would be
"Lord" (Lat *dominus*; OE *dryhten*). In such instances I follow
Æthelwold's translation practice, but after this I do not note his
alterations.

[14] *He . . . himself*: translating *RB 1980* Prol. 32, *"Qui gloriatur,
in Domino glorietur"* (*"He who boasts should make his boast in the
Lord"*).

*Matt 7:24-25
came, *winds blew and struck forcefully against that house, and it did not fall because it was founded on solid stone.**

35The Lord, working every good and replenishing and strengthening his holy ones, waits to see whether or not we wish to fulfill his teaching in our works. 36In order to remedy our sins, our days in this life are granted as a truce, 37as the apostle says: *Do you not* *Rom 2:4 *know that God's patience calls you to repentance?** 38Truly, the merciful Lord says, *I do not desire the death of the* *Ezek 33:11 *sinner, but that he would convert and have life.**

39Now that we have asked our Lord who may dwell in his tent, we have heard his precepts for meriting this. If we fulfill that service well, <we will become heirs of the Kingdom of heaven>. 40Therefore we must prepare our hearts and our entire bodies for battle and for the obedience of holy supplications.[15] 41So that we might not continue in our human frailty, we must eagerly ask the Lord that he help us to fulfill his precepts with his grace. 42And if we wish to avoid the torment of hell's punishment and come to eternal life, 43then, while we are able, while we dwell in this body and can fulfill all these aforesaid teachings by the light of life, 44we must hasten and quicken our pace so that we may advance to life in eternity.

45I wish therefore to set forth the labors and observances required for this lordly service.[16] 46Though

---

[15] The manuscripts have OE *to hyrsumnesse halȝra ȝebeda* for *RB 1980* Prol. 40, "sanctae praeceptorum oboedientiae" ("of holy obedience to his instructions"). *ȝebeda* means "prayers" or "supplications," while *ȝebodu* ("commands," "precepts") would be expected here (as *ȝeboda* translated *praecepta* in *RB 1980* Prol. 1), though the adjective has also been transferred. This could be a scribal error, a variant in Æthelwold's Latin manuscript(s) of the Rule, or a refashioning of the line to emphasize the role of prayer in monastic life.

[16] "the . . . service": translating *RB 1980* Prol. 45, "dominici schola servitii" ("a school for the Lord's service"). While Æthelwold's translation retains the Rule's emphasis on "the monas-

there are some things set out in this rule, <which is a guide on our journey to Christ>, that are a little severe and taught strenuously [47]in order to direct discretion, to remedy sin, and to ensure the observance of true unity, [48]do not be frightened and dismayed on this account. Nor should you abandon the path of your salvation on account of sloth. The beginning of this path, <which leads to Christ>, cannot be begun without some distress at its outset. [49]But then the dignity of these holy virtues and the practice of this holy life will become easy and light through faith, though they seemed difficult and distressful before.[17] The path is ample and slopes downward that leads to death and the punishments of hell; that which leads to life and the Kingdom of heaven is narrow and steep.* We take the latter path with an untroubled mind, good and

*see Matt 7:13–14

---

tery [as] the place where Christ continues to teach his disciples the baptismal renunciation of sin and the ways that lead to the repose of eternal life" in a corporate setting (see n. to *RB 1980* Prol. 45), it also dispenses with the much-admired metaphor of Lat *schola* ("school").

[17] "light through faith": in this and the surrounding sentences, Æthelwold has departed significantly from *RB 1980*, and the word translated as "light through faith," OE *leafleoht*, is attested only here in the Old English corpus. It appears to be a compound derived from the words *leaf* ("faith") and *leoht* ("light"), though it is not formed in the usual manner of compounding in Old English and its meaning is not readily apparent given its place in the translation. Though Gretsch suggests an emendation to *leofleoht* ("agreeably easy") in IF (120–21), I have chosen to follow the manuscripts' readings. Gretsch's argument has merit—especially considering that "agreeably easy" would be a more synonymous doublet with OE *eaþe* ("easy") and so closer to Old English authors' general use of doublets—but I follow what Anglo-Saxon and later readers would have found in the manuscripts, as every manuscript offers the reading *leafleoht*. That is, even if it is not Æthelwold's original word, it is what most readers of the manuscripts of the Old English Rule for centuries would have read and wrestled with, so I let it stand.

joyful thoughts, and the fulfillment of God's precepts. [50]Thus we may continue on in Christ's instruction and teaching in the monastery. Imitating him, let us suffer with patience in difficulties and in persecution. Then we may be permitted to possess fellowship in his Kingdom and have joy with him.[18]

---

[18] Omitting the *receptus* and *purus* reading "Amen" found in *RB 1980* Prol. 50. This final paragraph is by far the point in RB's Prologue at which Æthelwold translates most loosely; the general elements of RB are present, but the constructions and rhetoric stray heavily from the original.

Here Begin the Chapters on the Monastic Life.[19]

---

[19] The literal rendering of Æthelwold's title would be "Here Begin the Chapters of the Monasteries."

[20] Schröer's edition reproduces the manuscript reading, which gives chapter VIII as "VIII. Concerning the Twelve Steps of Complete Humility," thus displacing the chapter numbers throughout the rest of the current table of contents. To reduce confusion, I have not reproduced this numbering.

Here End the Chapters.

---

[21] "of the Children": not found in the main text's chapter heading.

[22] Omitting from the chapter heading of the main text, "and Their Servants."

I. Concerning the Kinds of Monks

[1]There are four kinds of monks. [2]The first are those who live in a monastery,[1] that is, those who undertake their battle under a rule and an abbot's teaching.

[3]The second kind is the anchorites, <that is, those who dwell in the wilderness>. They do not possess a new fervor; [4]rather, they have learned through their long practice of the monastic life how they, standing alone, can fight against the devil, the sins of their flesh, and their thoughts [5]with the help of God and the encouragement of their brothers.[2]

[6]The third kind is the foulest of all monks: those who depend on their own judgment.[3] They are not tried by the teaching of a rule and a teacher *as gold is tried by fire;*[4]* rather, they melt and grow weak like lead <when they are tempted>, [7]and they set all their hope in worldly things, as if they could deceive almighty God with their tonsure and their appearance as monks. [8]They live two or three together, and sometimes alone, not enclosed in God's flock but deluded

*Prov 27:21

---

[1] A fairly literal rendering of the OE compound noun *mynstermann* ("a person who lives in a monastery"), used to translate *RB 1980* 1.2, *coenobita*, in order to demonstrate Æthelwold's effort to convey the meaning of the original in a transparent manner for those not familiar with Latin terminology.

[2] This sentence condenses *RB 1980* 1.3-5.

[3] A fairly literal rendering of the OE compound noun *sylfdema*, which Æthelwold uses for a transparent translation of *RB 1980* 1.6, *sarabaita*.

[4] "*as . . . fire*": translating *RB 1980* 1.6, "*sicut aurum fornacis*" ("as gold is tried in a furnace"). Æthelwold uses OE *heorð* (literally a "hearth" or "fireplace") for Vulgate *fornax* ("furnace"), which implies a cultural translation of the biblical word. However, since in some cases *heorð* refers to fire itself, I have used this word as a compromise to get closer to the Latin sense of "the teaching of a rule and a teacher," translating and expanding the *receptus* reading of "experientia magistri/magisterii" ("experience of a teacher") instead of *RB 1980* 1.6, "experientia magistra" ("with no experience to guide them").

by their own desires. Their law is the desire of their idle will. ⁹Whatever idleness they have recourse to and choose, that they reckon holy, and whatever displeases them—<though it be holy>—they dismiss as unlawful.

¹⁰The fourth kind of monk is named the "wide-wandering,"⁵ those who go throughout various countries all their lives and dwell for two or three days in the houses of various people.⁶ ¹¹Always vagabonds and unsettled, they fulfill and obey their own desires and their unlawful appetites.⁷ They are worse in every way than those who depend on their own judgment, <who hold their peace in one dwelling>.

¹²Concerning the miserable life of all these it is better to keep silent than to speak. ¹³We will therefore omit this and turn to the strongest kind, those who live in monasteries and arrange their way of life with the help of God.

II. What Kind of Man the Abbot Must Be

¹The abbot who is worthy of governing a monastery must always remember what he is called and fulfill his title of supremacy in his deeds. ²He is Christ's vicar <and holds the mark and place of Christ in the monastery>. Therefore he is called by [Christ's] own title, ³which the apostle affirms, saying, *You have received the spirit of adoption of children by which we call out*

---

⁵ A fairly literal rendering of the OE compound noun *wid-scriþul*, used to translate RB 1.10 *gyrovagum* in a transparent manner.

⁶ "the homes": translating *RB 1980* 1.10, "cellas" ("the [cells/] monasteries") as OE *husum* ("houses"), even though Old English has words for both "cells" and "monasteries."

⁷ "own desires": translating the *receptus* reading "propriis voluptatibus" ("own desires") instead of *RB 1980* 1.11, "propriis voluntatibus" ("own wills")

*Rom 8:15

"Abba"—that is, "Father."[8]* [4]Therefore the abbot should never teach or establish or command anything except God's commands. [5]Rather, his behest and teaching, the leaven of divine justice, should always be scattered upon the minds of his subordinates. [6]Let him be ever mindful that in God's fearful Judgment great consideration will be made of both his teaching and the obedience of his subordinates. [7]He ought to know also that, just like a careless shepherd,[9] he will be punished if the shepherd's superior —<that is, the Lord>—finds too little profit and usefulness among his flock. [8]And yet, if he protects his disobedient flock and his unhealthy [charges] with every care— that is, provides them with every remedy for sinful deeds—[9]at that Judgment he will be glad and free of worry,[10] saying with the prophet, *Your justice, Lord, I have not hidden in my heart; I have declared your truth and salvation,** yet they despised and rejected me.** [10]Therefore punishment and death will hold sway over the flock that was disobedient to his care.

*Ps 39 [40]:11

*Isa 1:2; Ezek
20:27

[11]Whoever receives the great title of abbot must earnestly govern and instruct those who are subordinate to him with a twofold teaching. [12]He must teach each good thing and holiness through good deeds more than through instruction with words, so that those with understanding may be reminded of God's will through instruction with words and that those lacking understanding, strengthened and goaded on by good

---

[8] Throughout the text, words in brackets are supplied to clarify syntax or meaning in particulary ambiguous phrases.

[9] Instead of calling the abbot a Lat *pastor* ("shepherd") via metaphor as in *RB 1980* 2.7, Æthelwold compares him to an OE *ȝymeleas hyrde* ("careless shepherd") via simile, perhaps to emphasize the resonance of this passage with the contrast between the good Shepherd and the hireling in John 10:11-18 and the unacceptable shepherds of Israel of Ezek 34:1-10.

[10] "he . . . worry": translating the *receptus* reading "erit liber/ liber erit" ("will be free") instead of *RB 1980* 2.8, "erit ut" ("will be") followed by a clause.

deeds, may imitate him. [13]All that he forbids and detests before his disciples he must shun in his own works. If he teaches them well and then gives them an example of evil in his works, he will be severely punished.[11] [14]And the Lord will call out to that sinful one through his prophet, *Why do you speak about my justice, and why do you take my commands into your mouth? Truly you hate right teaching and cast away my words behind you.** [15]*You saw the little mote in your brother's eye and did not see the great pole in your own eye.*[12]* <That signifies, you reproved the lesser sins in your disciples and would not [reprove] the greater ones in yourself.>[13]

*Ps 49 [50]:16-17
*Matt 7:3

[16]The abbot should not discriminate by rank in the monastery—<that is, he should not honor someone on account of his birth or age or any other reason, except for that one's fear of God and discretion of true wisdom alone>. [17]Nor should he love one more than another, unless he find a particular person better in good deeds and in obedience. [18]Nor should he set the nobly born before those born as slaves—if the one born as a slave was in the monastery earlier—unless

---

[11] "he will be severely punished": replacing *RB 1980* 2.13, "*ne aliis praedicans ipse reprobus inveniatur*" ("*lest after preaching to others, he himself be found reprobate*" [1 Cor 9:27]).

[12] "You . . . own eye": translating *RB 1980* 2.15, "*et: Qui in fratris tui oculo festucam videbas, in tuo trabem non vidisti*" ("And also this: *How is it that you can see a splinter in your brother's eye, and never notice the plank in your own?*").

[13] "That . . . yourself": It seems likely that Æthelwold has drawn on Smaragdus, Expositio 2.15 (68; Comm 133–34) for this comment; he interprets this quotation from Matthew at length in this manner, e.g., "In fratris sui oculo festucam abbas videt, sed in suo trabem non videt, quando vel minimas subiectorum suorum culpas publice et exaggerando iudicat, et sua maiora parvipendens occultat et emendare dissimulat" ("The abbot sees the speck in his brother's eyes but does not see the beam in his own when he publicly and with some exaggeration judges the very minor faults of his subjects yet thinks little of his own greater faults, which he hides and neglects to amend").

he does it for a particular reason.[14] [19]<That is, if in some godly skill the nobly born person surpasses the one who is not nobly born, he may be honored more than the one who is not nobly born on account of his merits. This is not to be done on account of one's birth alone, but for the right ordering of the whole monastery, so that he who is greater in merit before God may be granted a greater position and seat. Let him be of whatever birth or date of entry into monastic life as he is: unless he surpasses another in his merit, he should be honored with the station and seat that corresponds to his entry into monastic life>.[15] [20]*For*

---

[14] "for a particular reason": translating the *receptus* reading "aliqua rationabilis causa" instead of *RB 1980* 2.18, "alia rationabilis causa" ("except for some other good reason"), and omitting "rationabilis."

[15] "That . . . life": This passage greatly expands on *RB 1980* 2.19, which these lines replace, and roughly corresponds to Smaragdus, Expositio 2.19 (69; Comm 135): "Non propterea quia ingenuus est, aut superiorem ordinis teneat locum aut praepositi vel decani teneat ministerium, *nisi alia rationabilis causa existat*. Rationabilis causa est, ut is qui in ecclesia melius potest cantare et legere vel omne officium implere, tali congruo consituatur loco ut digne possit illud implere officium . . . . Sed si rationabilis exigit causa, et in ordine constituatur superior et in ministerio prior . . . . *Sin autem propria teneant loca*, id est propter potentiae vel ingenuitatis dignitatem alter non praeponatur alteri, sed unusquisque in quo ordinis loco venit in ipso permaneat" ("Not because he is freeborn is someone either to hold a higher place in community order or hold the ministry of prior or dean, *unless there be another reasonable cause*. A reasonable cause would be, for example, that he who can sing and read better in church, and fulfill every office, should be put in such a fitting place that he can worthily fulfill that office . . . . But if a reasonable cause requires it, let him be put both higher in order and prior in ministry . . . . *Otherwise they are to keep their own places*, that is, one is not to be put before another on account of the dignity of his power and his being freeborn, but each one is to remain in the very place of the order in which he came"). It seems that Æthelwold wanted to emphasize the relationships in the monastery between religious of different rank within the specific social structure of Anglo-Saxon England.

whether slave or free, we are all one in Christ,* and we have received the same service under one God.[16] *For with God there is no respect of rank*[17]* [21]—that is, of power or age—except in merit alone.[18] [22][The abbot] must completely love his subordinates equally, and there must be for all one discipline and one teaching according to the nature of their merits.

[23]In his teaching the abbot must always hold to the apostle's saying, in which he says, *Rebuke, punish, entreat, and reproach.*[19]* [24]He must mingle severity with mildness,[20] so that he may show his fatherly severity and his gracious love. [25]That is, he must rebuke the restless and hard-hearted and punish and entreat the obedient, the docile, and the patient, so that they may do better and better. And he must rebuke the careless and proud either with words or with deeds.[21] [26]He must not delay or feign as if he were unaware, but as soon as he perceives something sinful he must cut it

*Gal 3:28;
Eph 6:8

*Rom 2:11

*2 Tim 4:2

---

[16] Æthelwold again removes a martial connotation, this time replacing *RB 1980* 2.20, "servitutis militiam" with OE *þeowdom* ("service").

[17] "*For . . . rank*": translating *RB 1980* 2.20, "quia *non est apud Deum personarum acceptio*" ("for *God shows no partiality among persons*").

[18] "that . . . alone": translating *RB 1980* 2.21.

[19] "*Rebuke . . . reproach*": translating *RB 1980* 2.23, "*Argue, obsecra, increpa*" ("*Use argument, appeal, reproof*"). Here Æthelwold introduces a fourth term (OE *witna*, "punish") to Paul's tripartite list and uses the OE verb *þreagan* to translate Lat *arguere*, the former being limited to the harsher connotation of "rebuke," etc. rather than the more neutral possible connotations of the latter. This reworking of the passage from 2 Tim does seem to make the verse harsher than the biblical and the Rule's usage.

[20] "He . . . mildness": replacing *RB 1980* 2.24, "id est, miscens temporibus tempora, terroribus blandimenta, dirum magistri" ("This means that he must vary with circumstances, threatening and coaxing by turns, stern as a task master") with a translation of "Miscenda ergo est lenitas cum seueritate," from Gregory, Reg past II.6 via Smaragdus, Expositio 2.24 (72; Comm 139).

[21] "That . . . deeds": reshaping *RB 1980* 2.25 while not removing or adding much.

*see 1 Sam
2:11–4:18

off. He must remember the peril of Eli, the priest of
Shiloh.* [27]<If they misbehave>, he must reprove good
men with words [28]and evil men with blows and bodily
chastening. He must remember that it is written, *The*

*Prov 29:19

foolish person cannot be corrected with words,* [29]and again
in another place, *Strike your son with a rod, and you will*

*Prov 23:14

free his soul from death.*

[30]The abbot must always recall that it is written that
more will be asked from the person to whom more is
entrusted.[22] [31]He must remember that it is with great
difficulty that he undertakes leadership—that is, that
he must direct and rule the souls of different people,[23]
some with coaxing, some with rebuke, some with
teaching. [32]Not only must he always desire that the
flock entrusted to him not diminish, but also that he
may rejoice in the fruits of their good works.[24] [33-34]He
should not consider lightly that he will have to render
an account on Judgment Day of all those for whom
he has undertaken the direction of souls.[25] [35]He must
not complain or lament concerning [a lack of] worldly
goods, for it is written: *Seek first the kingdom of God and*

*Matt 6:3

his justice, and he will give you all that you need.[26]* [36]And
again it is written, *There is no lack for those who fear God*

---

[22] "The abbot . . . entrusted": omitting *RB 1980* 2.30, "quod
est, meminere quod dicitur, et scire" ("what he is and remember
what he is called, aware that").

[23] "direct . . . and . . . rule": replacing *RB 1980* 2.31, "regere
. . . et . . . servire" ("directing . . . and serving").

[24] "Not . . . desire that," replacing *RB 1980* 2.32, "et secundum
uniuscuisque qualitatem vel intellegentiam, ita se omnibus
conformet et aptet ut" ("He must so accommodate and adapt
himself to each one's character and intelligence that").

[25] "He . . . souls": compressing *RB 1980* 2.34 and 2.35 and
retaining more of the latter.

[26] "Seek . . . need": translating *RB 1980* 2.35, "*Primum quaerite
regnum Dei et iustitiam eius, et haec omnia adicientur vobis*" ("*Seek
first the kingdom of God and his justice, and all these things will be
given you as well*").

properly.[27]* [37]The abbot must also know that he who   *Ps 33 [34]:10
accepts the direction of souls must prepare himself for
Judgment in the power of Judgment Day. [38]There he
must render an account of all those he accepted and
of his own soul.[28]

III. Concerning How to Summon the Whole Community for Important Counsel

[1]As often as any important matter is to be done in
the monastery, the abbot will summon the whole community and tell all those gathered what needs to be
considered. [2]And, hearing their counsel, he will consider it in his own mind and do what seems best to
him. [3]We command that the whole community should
be summoned for counsel, because often God reveals
to the youngest that which is best.[29] [4]The brothers take
counsel and so give their advice, with all humility and
submission, so that no one presumes to defend his
own advice with obstinacy. [5]Rather, every counsel
stands in the abbot's judgment. He will do what seems
best and most salutary,[30] and they in turn will eagerly
obey him. [6]But even as it is befitting that the younger
obey the older, so it is befitting that the elder—<that
is, the abbot>—very justly and prudently arrange and
settle common matters.

---

[27] *"There . . . properly"*: translating *RB 1980* 2.36, *"Nihil deest
timentibus eum"* ("Those who fear him lack nothing").

[28] "The abbot . . . own soul": compressing *RB 1980* 2.37 and
2.38 and omitting *RB 1980* 2.39-40.

[29] "Youngest" and "best": replacing the comparatives
"iuniori" ("younger") and "melius" ("better") found in *RB 1980*
3.3 with superlatives.

[30] "Best" and "most salutary": replacing the comparative
"salubrius" ("salutary, beneficial") found in *RB 1980* 3.5 with
the superlative.

[7]In every matter they must hold the rule as their teacher, and no one should turn from it through any presumption. [8]Nor should anyone desire to follow his own will. [9]Nor again shall anyone presume to say anything harsh against his abbot, either within the monastery or without.[31] [10]If someone does, then he must undergo the discipline of the rule's teaching.[32] [11]Yet the abbot should know that everything he does should be done with the fear of God and in observance of the rule, since without a doubt he must render an account of all his judgments before the just Judge on Judgment Day.

[12]If a less important matter needs to be considered, then he has the counsel of the oldest men, [13]for it is written, *All that you do, do it with counsel, and you will not repent of* it.[33]*

*Sir 32:24

[31] "Anything harsh . . . , either within . . . without": translating the *receptus* reading "proterve intus aut foris monasterium" (or one of the other very close variants) instead of *RB 1980* 3.9, "proterve aut foris monasterium" ("defiantly, or outside the monastery"); see n. to *RB 1980* 3.9.

[32] "the discipline of the rule's teaching": translating Æthelwold's awkward (to us?) translation of Lat "regulari disciplinae" ("to the regular discipline") as OE *þære steore reȝollicre lare*. *Disciplina regularis* is normally translated in modern English as "the discipline of the rule" (making the adjective *regularis* into a genitive noun); had Æthelwold translated this Latin phrase as *þære steore reȝollicre* or as *þære reȝollicre lare* I would have felt comfortable translating his Old English as the accepted modern English "discipline of the rule." However, since his translation adds another word to the Latin phrase, it appears that he intended to spell out precisely what he wanted his audience to read or hear, hence "the discipline of the rule's teaching." See Kenneth Hein, "Appendix 4: The Disciplinary Measures in the Rule of Benedict," in Fry, 415–36, here 434–35.

[33] "All . . . . of it": translating *RB 1980* 3.13, "*Omnia fac cum consilio et post factum non paeniteberis*" ("*Do everything with counsel and you will not be sorry afterward*").

IV. Concerning the Tools for Good Works

¹First one must *love God with all one's heart and all one's spirit, and all one's strength,* ²and after this *one's neighbor as oneself.*³⁴‡ ³One must *not kill,* ⁴*nor have illicit intercourse,* ⁵*nor steal,* ⁶*nor unlawfully desire,** ⁷*nor bear false witness.*° ⁸Rather, one *must honor everyone*∞ ⁹and *not do to others what he does not want others to do to him.*◊

¹⁰One *must deny one's own desires and follow Christ's teaching;*³⁵* ¹¹everyone must purify *his body*—that is, *subdue* it with restraint;³⁶† ¹²one must not <greedily> love luxuries, ¹³but rather love fasting. ¹⁴One must encourage the poor ¹⁵and *clothe the naked,* ¹⁶*visit the sick,** ¹⁷and bury the dead, ¹⁸help the troubled, ¹⁹and console the sorrowing.

²⁰Everyone must make himself indifferent to worldly longings ²¹and set nothing before the love of Christ. ²²One must not act in anger ²³but hold onto irascibility only temporarily,³⁷ ²⁴nor have deceit in his heart, ²⁵nor give a false sign of peace, ²⁶nor neglect charity.³⁸ ²⁷One must not swear, lest one forswear, ²⁸and must always bring forth truth from one's heart and mouth.

‡Matt 22:37-39;
Mark 12:30-31;
Luke 10:27
*Rom 13:9
°Matt 19:18;
Mark 10:19;
Luke 18:20
∞1 Pet 2:17
◊Tob 4:16; Matt 7:12; Luke 6:31
*Matt 16:24;
Luke 9:23
†cf. 1 Cor 9:27

*Matt 25:36

---

³⁴ "one . . . *oneself*": translating *RB 1980* 4.1-2, "*Dominum Deum diligere ex toto corde, tota anima, tota virtute; deinde proximum tamquam seipsum*" ("*love the Lord God with your whole heart, your whole soul and all your strength, and love your neighbor as yourself*"). "one must": translating the imperatives in *RB 1980* 4 as the impersonal construction *(ne) sceal mon* ("one must [not]") and *(ne) he sceal* ("he must [not]"), lending a proverbial tone to RB's immediacy.

³⁵ "*Christ's* teaching": translating *RB 1980* 4.10, "*Christum*" ("*Christ*").

³⁶ "everyone . . . restraint": translating *RB 1980* 4.11, "*Corpus castigare*" ("*discipline your body*").

³⁷ "but . . . temporarily": replacing the negative command of *RB 1980* 4.23, "*iracundiae tempus non reservare*" ("or nurse a grudge") with a positive.

³⁸ Here, as elsewhere in the Old English corpus, *soþ lufu* ("true love") translates Lat *caritas* ("charity").

*1 Thess 5:15;
1 Pet 3:9

*Matt 5:44;
Luke 6:27

*Matt 5:10

*Titus 1:7; 1 Tim
3:3
*Rom 12:11

²⁹One must *not return injury for injury*,* ³⁰nor do any harm to anyone; rather, when someone does injury to him, one must bear it patiently. ³¹One must *love his enemy* <for the love of God>.* ³²One must not curse those who curse, but rather bless them. ³³One must *humbly endure persecution for the sake of righteousness*.³⁹*

³⁴One must *not be proud*, ³⁵*eager for drink*,* ³⁶gluttonous, ³⁷*given to sleep*, ³⁸*lazy*,* ³⁹given to grumbling, ⁴⁰nor given to speaking ill of others.

⁴¹But he must place all his hope in God. ⁴²When he does something good he must completely give God the credit, ⁴³and when he does something evil he must know that it comes from himself.

⁴⁴He must always give thought to Judgment Day, ⁴⁵must always fear the punishments of hell ⁴⁶and yearn for eternal life with all eagerness, ⁴⁷and each day he must think on his death. ⁴⁸At every hour he must take heed <that his works are good and> ⁴⁹consider that in no place is he hidden from God, but everywhere [God] sees him. ⁵⁰When evil thoughts come into his mind, he must immediately dash them against Christ and confess them to his spiritual master. <To dash them against Christ, he remembers Christ's passion and his miracles—with those thoughts he puts the evil ones to flight>. ⁵¹His mouth he must keep from every wickedness and harmful words, ⁵²and he must not speak many idle words ⁵³or those that produce laughter. ⁵⁴He must not love laughter.

⁵⁵He must willingly listen to holy reading ⁵⁶and be often at prayer. ⁵⁷He must daily confess his past evil deeds to God with tears ⁵⁸and eagerly amend them.

---

³⁹ "*humbly . . . righteousness*": translating *RB 1980* 4.33, "*Persecutionem pro iustitia sustinere*" ("*Endure persecution for the sake of justice*").

[59]He must *not follow his bodily desires,*[40]* [60]must detest his own will, [61]and must obey the commands of his abbot in all things, even if it is the case that [the abbot] acts—as he should not—worse than he teaches.[41] They must remember the Lord's saying in which he says, *Do what they say, not what they do.** *Gal 5:16

*Matt 23:3

[62]Let him not <be eager for praise nor> desire that his deeds be called holy before they are. Rather, let him take mind that they may be truly called so. [63]He must fulfill God's commands daily with good deeds [64]and love his chastity. [65]He must hate no one, [66]nor harbor jealousy [67]or envy,[42] [68]nor love strife. [69]He must flee arrogance, [70]honor his elders, [71]and love the young. [72]Out of love for God they must pray for their enemies; [73]before the sun sets they must make peace with those with whom they have had disagreements.[43]

[74]And he must never despair of God's mercy.

[75]Now these are the tools <and building materials> of the spiritual craft. [76]When we have used them day and night without ceasing and return them on Judgment Day, the reward the Lord will give us will be [the

---

[40] "not follow his bodily desires": translating *RB 1980* 4.59, "Desideria carnis non efficere" ("Do not gratify the promptings of the flesh").

[41] "worse than he teaches": translating *RB 1980* 4.61, "ipse aliter . . . agat" ("even if his own conduct . . . be at odds with what he says").

[42] "nor harbor jealousy or envy": translating the *receptus* and *interpolatus* reading "zelum et invidiam non habere" instead of *RB 1980* 4.66-67, "zelum non habere, invidiam non exercere" ("[harbor not] jealousy of anyone, and do nothing out of envy").

[43] "with . . . disagreements": translating the *receptus* reading "cum discordantibus" instead of *RB 1980* 4.73, "cum discordante" ("with him with whom you have had a dispute" [my translation]). In this sentence the pronouns and verbs shift from singular, as in the rest of the chapter, to plural, presumably reflecting the interpersonal nature of these precepts; this shift is not present in Benedict's Latin.

one] he himself promised,[44] that is, [77]*What the human eye—despite its greatness—has not seen, what the human ear has not heard, what has not arisen in the human heart,*

*1 Cor 2:9

that God has prepared for all those who love him.[45]*

[78]He must observe all this service and work at it eagerly in the enclosure of the monastery and the community's stability.

V. Concerning Obedience

[1]The first step of humility is obedience without delay. [2]This is fitting for those who consider nothing more [worthy of being] loved than <almighty> Christ. [3]They observe this [obedience] on account of their promise of holy service, the fear of hell, or the glory of eternal life. [4]As soon as their elder commands anything, they fulfill [that order] without delay, as if it were commanded by God himself. [5]Concerning such disciples the Lord says, *When he heard me with his ears*

*Ps 17 [18]:45

*he obeyed me.** [6]Again, he tells teachers, *He who hears*

*Luke 10:16

you hears me, and he who mishears you mishears me.[46]* [7]Such disciples, as soon as something is commanded, earnestly cast away their own will [8]and lay aside whatever business they have in hand unfinished. [9]With ready obedience their feet follow that commanding voice in their works. And as if in a glance,[47]

---

[44] "he himself": translating the *receptus* and *purus* reading "ipse" instead of *RB 1980* 4.76, "illa."

[45] "What . . . him": translating *RB 1980* 4.77, "*Quod oculus non vidit nec auris audivit, quae praeparavit Deus his qui diligunt illum*" ("*What the eye has not seen nor the ear heard, God has prepared for those who love him*"). "what . . . heart": translating the *receptus* reading "nec in cor hominis ascendit," which *RB 1980* omits.

[46] "He . . . mishears me": translating *RB 1980* 5.6, "*Qui vos audit me audit*" ("*Whoever listens to you, listens to me*").

[47] "a glance": this translates the variant reading *anre berhthwile* from Schröer's apparatus instead of his text's *are berhthwile*, the former of which is closer to *RB 1980* 5.9, "uno momento" ("at the same moment").

the behest of the master and the work of the disciple are promptly completed together in the fear of God.

¹⁰In such disciples dwells a love for the course to eternal life, ¹¹since they choose the narrow path, concerning which the Savior says, *Narrow and strict is the way that leads to life*⁴⁸*—that is, he does not live by his own judgment, nor does he obey his own desires.⁴⁹ ¹²Rather, he acts according to another's judgment and behest and ever desires to dwell in the monastery, so that the abbot may guide and teach him. ¹³Without doubt, such disciples imitate that saying that the Lord said concerning himself: *I have come not that I may work my own will, but that of him who sent me here.** ·Matt 7:14

·John 6:38

¹⁴This very obedience will be acceptable to God and pleasant to people if their compliance is done without fear, sloth, or lukewarmness, without grumbling or an unwilling answer. ¹⁵Truly, the obedience given to superiors is given for God. He himself truly said, *He who hears you, hears me.** ¹⁶Subordinate disciples must listen to their superiors with good minds and joyful thoughts, for without doubt *God loves a joyful servant* <and hates the gloomy>.⁵⁰* ¹⁷Indeed, though some disciple fulfills his superior's commands in his work, if he grumbles about it with his mouth or complains in his mind, ¹⁸[this work] will not be acceptable to God, whose sight penetrates each person's heart. ¹⁹Rather, he will not receive a reward <from God> for such a deed. On the contrary, eternal punishment is set in store for the one who murmurs <and so disobeys God>, unless he amend <his evil thought with full repentance>. ·Luke 10:16

·2 Cor 9:7

⁴⁸ *"Narrow and . . . to life"*: translating *RB 1980* 5.11, *"Angusta via est quae ducit ad vitam"* (*"Narrow is the road that leads to life"*).

⁴⁹ "his own desires": translating the *receptus* reading "desideriis suis" instead of *RB 1980* 5.12, "desideriis suis et voluptatibus" ("to their whims and appetites").

⁵⁰ *"servant"*: translating *RB 1980* 5.16, "datorem" ("giver").

VI. Concerning Silence

¹Let us do as the prophet reminds us, saying, *I said that I have watched over my ways, that I might not sin with my tongue. I have set a guard over my mouth. I kept silence and ceased even from good words.** ²With these words the holy prophet shows that we must cease from idle words in view of punishment for sins. If he often refrains from good words <because of the power of silence>, he must earnestly refrain from idle words. ³Permission to speak on holy discourses and the edification of the soul should seldom be given, even to mature disciples, on account of the importance of silence.⁵¹ ⁴For it is written <in the holy books>, *In much speech sin will not be avoided.** ⁵And again it is written, *Death and life are in the power of the tongue.*⁵²* ⁶Truly, the teacher ought to speak and teach, while the disciple ought to keep silence and listen.

⁷Therefore, if anyone is to ask something of his superior, he should ask with all humility, a submissive will, and great reverence.⁵³ He should not speak more than profits him.⁵⁴ ⁸Buffoonery, idle words, and words that lead to laughter we condemn and forbid in every place by means of an eternal enclosure;⁵⁵ I withhold

*Ps 38 [39]:2-3

*Prov 10:19
*Prov 18:21

---

⁵¹ "on holy . . . soul": free translation of *RB 1980* 6.3, "de bonis et sanctis et aedificationum eloquiis" ("how good or holy or constructive their talk").

⁵² "*power*": translating OE *handa* (literally "hands"), which literally translates *RB 1980* 6.5, Lat "manibus" ("hands").

⁵³ "a . . . reverence": expanding *RB 1980* 6.7, "subiectione reverentiae" ("respectful submission").

⁵⁴ "He . . . him": translating the *receptus* reading "ne videatur plus loqui quam expedit," which *RB 1980* omits.

⁵⁵ "with an eternal enclosure": translating OE *ecum loce*, which literally translates *RB 1980* 6.8, Lat "aeterna clausura" ("eternal enclosure"), a phrase that refers to enclosure and envisions the mouth as a sort of door to the inner cloister; cf. n. to *RB 1980* 6.8. RB plays on this image of the enclosure in the following clause, withholding permission for the disciple to "open" (Lat *aperire*) his mouth to the condemned kinds of speech. Æthel-

permission for any disciple to open his mouth for such speech.

VII. Concerning Humility

¹Divine Scripture exhorts us to humility, saying, *Whoever exalts himself will be condemned, and whoever condemns himself with humility, he will be lifted up with honor.*⁵⁶* ²In these words it is shown that every exaltation springs from a kind of pride. ³The prophet warns against this vice, saying, *Lord, my heart is not exalted nor my eyes turned upward; I have not walked among great things nor extravagantly boasted with pomp.*⁵⁷* ⁴And why? *If I did not consider myself humbly, but exalted my spirit in pride, you would repay me, Lord, with a bitter reward, just as a mother repays her child when she draws it from sucking at her breasts.*⁵⁸*

*Luke 14:11; 18:14

*Ps 130 [131]:1

*Ps 130 [131]:2

---

wold, by maintaining the literal image of the "eternal enclosure" in his translation, is able to maintain the complementary image of forbidding the disciple to "open" (OE *ontyne*) his mouth, which more idiomatic translations forfeit.

⁵⁶ "Whoever . . . *honor*": translating *RB 1980* 7.1, "*Omnis qui se exaltat humiliabitur et qui se humiliat exaltabitur*" ("*Whoever exalts himself shall be humbled, and whoever humbles himself shall be exalted*"). Here Æthelwold uses the same OE verb, *geneoþerian*, to translate Lat *humiliare* that he used to translate *damnare* in the last sentence of chapter VI. This usage blunts the parallelism of the gospel passage but makes a more forceful emphasis on the necessity of humility.

⁵⁷ "Lord . . . *pomp*": translating *RB 1980* 7.3, "*Domine, non est exaltatum cor meum neque elati sunt oculi mei, neque ambulavi in magnis neque in mirabilibus super me*" ("*O Lord, my heart is not exalted; my eyes are not lifted up and I have not walked in the ways of the great nor gone after marvels beyond me*").

⁵⁸ "If . . . *breasts*": translating *RB 1980* 7.4, "*si non humiliter sentiebam, si exaltavi animam meam?—sicut ablactatum super matrem suam, ita retribues in animam meam*" ("*If I had not a humble spirit, but were exalted instead, then you would treat me like a weaned child on its mother's lap*").

⁵Therefore, if we wish to reach the summit of lofty humility and intend to come quickly to that heavenly exaltation to which we ascend in the humility of this temporal life, ⁶then we must raise by our deeds that ladder upon which Jacob saw in a dream *angels both ascending and descending.**Gen 28:12 ⁷Without doubt, in this ascending and descending we are solely to understand that ascent to the Kingdom of heaven is merited by humility and forfeited by exaltation.⁵⁹ ⁸This ladder we raise signifies our life in this world,⁶⁰ which is raised to heaven by the Lord [if we possess] a humble heart. ⁹The sides of the ladder signify our body and soul. Upon these two sides—that is, upon the soul and the body—our divine vocation secures various steps of humility and discipline for our ascent.

VII.1 Concerning the Twelve Steps of Complete Humility⁶¹

¹⁰The first step of humility is that one have *fear of God* and continually set that sight *before his eyes,**Ps 35 [36]:2 not being forgetful but, rather, ever mindful of everything that the Lord commands. ¹¹One should also be mindful that those who despise his commands will fall into hell on account of their sins, ever considering the eter-

---

⁵⁹ "ascent . . . exaltation": freely translating *RB 1980* 7.7, "exaltatione descendere et humilitate ascendere" ("we descend by exaltation and ascend by humility").

⁶⁰ "This . . . world": Æthelwold again replaces Benedict's metaphor, this time explicitly linking the ladder and our earthly life by noting that the ladder "signifies" (OE *tacnað*) our life in this world. This strategy is carried forward in the following lines.

⁶¹ The OE headings for each step throughout chapter VII translate those that introduce each step in the manuscripts that include the Latin text of RB.

*Gen 28:12
*Ps 35 [36]:2

nal life *which God has prepared for all those who* fear
him.⁶²*   *1 Cor 2:9

¹²<Considering all this>, he should guard [himself]
from his sins and vices, whether of thought, speech,
or sight,⁶³ and speedily restrain his own desires and
the will of his flesh from every evil deed.⁶⁴ ¹³Every one
should know that he is always and at every moment
seen by the Lord in the heavens, that his deeds are
everywhere seen in the divine sight and reported by
the angels at every moment.

¹⁴The prophet shows us that God is present to our
thoughts when he says, *God searches the heart of men
and his emotions.*⁶⁵* ¹⁵Again he says, God *knows the*   *Ps 7:10
*thoughts of men.** ¹⁶Again he says, *Lord, you know my*   *Ps 93 [94]:11
*thoughts from afar,** ¹⁷and, *The thought of man will confess*   *Ps 138 [139]:3
*you.** ¹⁸To the extent that he is careful [to avoid] evil   *Ps 75 [76]:11
thoughts, the profitable brother calls out in his heart,
*I will be blameless before God if I guard myself from my
own sinfulness.*⁶⁶*   *Ps 17 [18]:24

---

⁶² *"which . . . him"*: translating *RB 1980* 7.11, "quae timentibus
Deum praeparata est animo suo semper evolvat" ("all who fear
God have eternal life awaiting them"), but altering the previous
clause's structure, to reflect Vulgate 1 Cor 2:9, "*quae praeparavit
Deus iis qui diligunt eum*" ("*which God has prepared for those who
love him*").

⁶³ "or sight": translating the *receptus* and *interpolatus* reading
"oculorum," which *RB 1980* 7.12 omits. Æthelwold also omits
RB 1980 7.12, "manuum, pedum" ("of hand or foot").

⁶⁴ "speedily . . . flesh": translating the *receptus* and *interpolatus* reading "desideria carnis amputare festinet," the last two
words of which *RB 1980* 7.12 omits.

⁶⁵ I translate OE *æddran* (literally "kidneys"), which translates
RB 1980 7.14, Lat "renes" (literally "kidneys"), as "emotions,"
since the kidneys were once thought of as the "seat of the feel-
ings or affections" (OED, s.v. *reins*).

⁶⁶ "*I will . . . sinfulness*": translating *RB 1980* 7.18, "*Tunc ero
immaculatus coram eo si observavero me ab iniquitate mea*" ("*I shall
be blameless in his sight if I guard myself from my own wickedness*").

¹⁹Our own will is forbidden to us when Holy Scripture says, *Turn from your desires.** ²⁰Again, in the Prayer we implore our Lord that his *will dwell* in us.⁶⁷* ²¹Concerning our deeds, we are earnestly instructed not to do our own will when Holy Scripture warns us, saying, *There are some paths which seem right to men which in the end plunge into the abyss of hell.*⁶⁸* ²²And we are brought to fear by that passage of Holy Scripture that says, *They are corrupted and made abominable in their desires.**

²³Concerning our fleshly desires, we should also know that the Lord is always present <and no part of our undertaking is hidden from him>. The prophet <shows us this>, calling out to God, *My whole will is present to you, Lord.*⁶⁹* ²⁵Concerning this, Holy Scripture reminds us, saying, *Do not go after your desires.**

²⁶Indeed, since *God's vision beholds both the good and the evil,*⁷⁰* ²⁷and *the Lord always looks down from heaven upon the sons of men that he may see whether any have understanding and seek God,** ²⁸and since day and night our works are reported to the Lord, <our Creator>, by the angels assigned to us, ²⁹this must serve as a great warning to us, dear brothers—as it says in the psalms: lest God at any time see us *falling* into evil and *turning*

*Sir 18:30
*Matt 6:10

*Prov 16:25

*Ps 13 [14]:1

*Ps 37 [38]:10
*Sir 18:30

*Prov 15:3

*Ps 13 [14]:2

---

⁶⁷ "his . . . us": translating *RB 1980* 7.20, "*fiat* illius *voluntas in* nobis" ("his *will be done* in us").

⁶⁸ "*There . . . hell*": this is a close translation of *RB 1980* 7.21's citation of Prov, which itself takes liberties.

⁶⁹ "*My . . . Lord*": translating *RB 1980* 7.23, "*Ante te est omne desiderium meum*" ("*All my desires are known to you*"). Here Æthelwold also omits *RB 1980* 7.24.

⁷⁰ "*God's . . . evil*": translating *RB 1980* 7.26, "*oculi Domini speculantur bonos et malos*" ("*the eyes of the Lord are watching the good and the wicked*"). It is possible that Æthelwold translates Lat "*oculi Domini*" ("*eyes of the Lord*") as OE *Godes gesyhða* ("*God's vision*"), borrowing from Smaragdus, *Expositio* 7.26 (175; Comm 285): "*Oculi Domini* respectio est divina . . ." ("*The eyes of the Lord* is the divine gaze . . .").

to naught.[71]* [30]And yet he spares us in this hour, because he is merciful. He waits for us to improve, lest he <send us away later>, saying, *This you did, and I kept silent.**

*Ps 13 [14]:3

*Ps 49 [50]:21

VII.2 Concerning the Second Step of Humility

[31]The second step of humility is that one does not love his own will or follow his own desires [32]but imitates in his deeds that saying of the Lord <that he says concerning himself>, *I did not come to do my own will but that of my heavenly Father.*[72]* [33]And again it is said, "Desire gains punishment; necessity provides a crown of glory"[73]—<that is, one should urge himself toward God and cast off his own desires>.[74]

*John 6:38

[71] *"falling . . . naught"*: translating *RB 1980* 7.29, *"declinantes in malo et inutiles factos"* (*"falling . . . into evil and so made worthless"*).

[72] *"I . . . Father"*: translating *RB 1980* 7.32, *"Non veni facere voluntatem meam, sed eius qui me misit"* (*"I have come not to do my own will, but the will of him who sent me"*).

[73] *"Desire"*: translating the *receptus* and *purus* reading *"voluptas"* instead of *RB 1980* 7.33, *"Voluntas"* (*"Consent"*). *"crown of glory"*: translating OE *wuldorbeah*—an expansion of *RB 1980* 7.33, *"coronam"* (*"crown"*)—a compound that is associated with Æthelwold's career and milieu, for which see Gretsch, IF 98–104.

[74] *"that . . . desires"*: though the clause is not a close translation, it seems that Æthelwold takes his lead from Smaragdus, Expositio 7.33 (178; Comm 288), "Hinc iterum dominus dicit, *Qui vult post me venire, abneget semetipsum, tollat crucem suam et sequatur me.* Quid est aliud semetipsum abnegare, nisi latam et spatiosam viam deserere et voluntates proprias odire? Quid est *tollat crucem suam et sequatur me,* nisi artam et angustam viam arripiat ubi pro me multas necessitates sustineat et sic ad gaudia perpetua me sequens veniat ubi aeternam coronam me donante recipiat?" ("Hence the Lord says again: *He who wants to come after me, let him deny himself and take up his cross and follow me.* What else is it to deny oneself, except to abandon the wide and

VII.3. Concerning the Third Step of Humility

³⁴The third step of humility is that one subject one-self to his superiors for the love of God with all humility,⁷⁵ imitating our Lord, concerning whom the apostle says, *He became obedient even to suffering the death of his will.*⁷⁶*

*Phil 2:8

VII.4. Concerning the Fourth Step of Humility

³⁵The fourth step of humility is that in this very obe-dience one is patient in difficult and adverse matters and in every injury, loving patience ³⁶and not growing weary, not forsaking his position nor turning away from God.⁷⁷ Concerning this, Holy Scripture reminds us, *He who perseveres to the end will be saved.** ³⁷And again it is said in Holy Scripture, *Strengthen your heart and wait patiently for the Lord*—<that is, endure all things, that God may support you>. ³⁸And again it is shown that the faithful must endure all the opposition of this world on account of their fear of God. Concern-ing their patience it is written,⁷⁸ *For you, Lord, we are afflicted with death all the day; we are marked for death as*

*Matt 10:22

*Ps 26 [27]:14

---

spacious way and to hate one's own wishes? What is *let him take up his cross and follow me,* except, Let him lay hold of the straight and narrow way, and there undergo many necessities for my sake; let him thus follow me and come to perpetual joys, to receive the eternal crown that I bestow?").

⁷⁵ "humility": translating *RB 1980* 7.34, "oboedientia" ("obe-dience").

⁷⁶ "*He . . . will*": translating *RB 1980* 7.34, "*Factus oboediens usque ad mortem*" ("*He became obedient even to death*").

⁷⁷ "not forsaking . . . God": expanding on *RB 1980* 7.36, "sus-tinens non lassescat vel discedat" ("and endures it without weakening or seeking escape").

⁷⁸ "Concerning . . . written": translating *RB 1980* 7.38, "dicit ex persona sufferentium" ("saying in the person of those who suffer").

sheep for slaughter.* [39]Yet they are free of care in that hope of divine reward, happily and continually calling out, *We have overcome in all things through him who loved us**—<that is, the Lord>. [40]Again, concerning that same patience, Holy Scripture says, *Lord, you have tried us; you have purified us in the trial of fire, just as silver is tried by fire. You have led us into a snare; you have set afflictions on our backs.*[79]* [41]Again, that same part of Holy Scripture shows us that we must be under the care of superiors—<that is, superiors who have authority over us>—saying, *You have set men over our heads.**

[42]You should also endure difficulties and injuries with patience through God's command,[80] fulfilling that saying <of the gospel> that says, *When you are struck on one cheek, turn the other as well; to the one who takes your tunic, give him your cloak as well; compelled to go one mile, go two freely.*[81]* That is to say, the man who *turns the other cheek* to the one who strikes him is he who *does good to the one who* has given him evil,[82]* who *blesses the one who curses him;*[83]* he *gives his cloak* to the one who *took his tunic* and *goes two miles* willingly after

*Rom 8:36; Ps 43 [44]:22

*Rom 8:37

*Ps 65 [66]:10-11

*Ps 65 [66]:12

*Matt 5:39-41; Luke 6:29

*Luke 6:27

*Luke 6:28; 1 Cor 4:12

---

[79] *"Lord . . . backs"*: translating *RB 1980* 7.40, *"Probasti nos, Deus, igne nos examinasti sicut igne examinatur argentum; induxisti nos in laqueum; posuisti tribulationes in dorso nostro"* (*"O God, you have tested us, you have tried us as silver is tried by fire; you have led us into a snare, you have placed afflictions on our back"*).

[80] *"endure . . . command"*: translating *RB 1980* 7.42, *"praeceptum Domini in adversis et iniuriis per patientiam adimplentes"* (*"those who are patient amid hardships and unjust treatment are fulfilling the Lord's command"*).

[81] *"When . . . freely"*: translating *RB 1980* 7.42, *"percussi in maxillam praebent et aliam, auferenti tunicam dimittunt et pallium, angariati miliario vadunt duo"* (*"When struck on one cheek, they turn the other; when deprived of their coat, they offer their cloak also; when pressed into service for one mile, they go two"*).

[82] *"does . . . evil"*: cf. Vulgate, *"benefacite his qui oderunt vos"* (*"do good to those who hate you"*).

[83] *"blesses . . . him"*: cf. Vulgate, *"benedicite maledicentibus vobis"* (*"bless those who curse you"*).

*Rom 12:21

he was *compelled to go one* whenever he is *overpowered by evil but turns from that evil to good.*[84]* [43]Such a man as this without doubt acts just as Paul said, that is, he patiently *endures false brothers** and *suffers persecution for the sake of righteousness,* and *blesses those who curse him.*[85]*

*2 Cor 11:26

*1 Cor 4:12;
1 Pet 3:14

VII.5. Concerning the Fifth Step of Humility

[44]The fifth step of humility is that he discloses to his abbot with a humble confession all of the thoughts that come into his heart and those evil deeds committed by him in secret. [45]Concerning this, Holy Scripture

---

[84] *"gives . . . good"*: cf. Vulgate, *"noli vinci a malo, sed vince in bono malum"* (*"Do not be overcome by sin, but overcome sin with good"*).

[85] *"that . . . patiently"*: freely translating Smaragdus, Expositio 7.42 (182; Comm 294), "Qui enim in iniuriis inrogatis non reddit malum pro malo, ille *maxillam* percutienti unam praebet *et aliam;* ille qui maledictum non reddit pro maledicto, *auferenti tunicam* dimittit *et pallium* ille qui non vincitur a malo sed vincit in bono malum, *angariati miliario* voluntarie pergit *duo.* Iste sine dubio talis patienter *cum Paulo falsos fratres substinet et maledicentes* benedicendo veraciter humilitatis implet praeceptum" ("The one who does not return evil for evil when made to suffer injustice, offers one and then *the other cheek* to the one who strikes him, does not repay curse with curse; *to someone who takes away [his] tunic [he] also surrenders [his] cloak,* is not overcome by evil but overcomes evil with good, of his own accord *goes two miles for the person who forces him to go one*—such a one as this without a doubt patiently *endures false brothers with Paul,* and by blessing *those who curse* him really fulfills the precept of humility"). While Æthelwold's version is very close to Smaragdus's, it should be noted that Æthelwold does not translate slavishly, even altering the sense of Smaragdus's "is not overcome by evil but overcomes evil with good" to "whenever he is *overpowered by evil but turns from that evil to good.*" *"suffers . . . him"*: cf. Vulgate *"maledicimur, et benedicimus: persecutionem patimur, et sustinemus"* (*"we are cursed, and we bless; we suffer persecution, and we endure"*). *"for the sake of righteousness"*: translating the *receptus* and *interpolatus* reading *"propter iustitiam"* (citing 1 Pet 3:14), which *RB 1980* 7.43 omits.

reminds us, saying, *Make known your way to the Lord—
<that is, your deeds>—and hope in him.*[86]* [46]And again
it says, *Confess to the Lord, for he is good; his mercy is
eternal.** [47]Again, the prophet says, *My sin I will make
known to the Lord, and my faults I have not concealed.* [48]*I
have said, against myself I will report my faults to the Lord,
and you have forgiven the wickedness of my heart.**

*Ps 36 [37]:5

*Ps 105 [106]:1;
Ps 117 [118]:1

*Ps 31 [32]:5

VII.6. Concerning the Sixth Step of Humility

[49]The sixth step of humility is that a monk is content
and agreeable, though he reckons himself poor and
unworthy, suffers only extreme treatment, and deems
himself to be the worst.[87] In all duties entrusted to him
he reckons himself a poor and unworthy workman
[50]and with the prophet calls out, *I was reduced to nothing, and I did not know; I have become like a beast before
you, and yet I am always with you.**

*Ps 72 [73]:22-23

VII.7. Concerning the Seventh Step of Humility

[51]The seventh step of humility is that a monk reckon
himself lower and more unworthy than any other.[88]
[52]He humbles himself and says with the prophet, *Truly,
I am a worm and no man, a reproach to men and an outcast
of the people.** [53]*I was exalted, [then] humbled and con-
founded.** [54]And again, *It is good for me that you have
humbled me, that I may learn your commands.**

*Ps 21 [22]:7
*Ps 87 [88]:16
*Ps 118 [119]:71,
73

---

[86] "that is, your deeds": addition borrowed from Smaragdus,
Expositio 7.45 (183; Comm 295), "Id est *revela . . .* actiones tuas"
("That is, *reveal* your actions"). Smaragdus here bases his com-
mentary on Prov 16:3.

[87] "though . . . worst": translating *RB 1980* 7.49, "omni vilitate
vel extremitate" ("with the lowest and most menial treatment").

[88] Omitting *RB 1980* 7.51, "non solum sua lingua pronuntiet,
sed etiam intimo cordis . . . affectu" ("not only admits with his
tongue, but is also . . . in his heart").

VII.8. Concerning the Eighth Step of Humility

[55]The eighth step of humility is that a monk does nothing except what the common rule of the monastery teaches, or the instruction set by the example of his superiors.[89]

VII.9. Concerning the Ninth Step of Humility

[56]The ninth step of humility is that a monk restrains his tongue from speech and, keeping silent, does not speak until asked [to do so], [57]concerning which Holy Scripture shows us, *In much speech, sin will not be avoided,** [58]and, *The talkative man will not prosper on the earth.**

*Prov 10:19
*Ps 139 [140]:12

VII.10. Concerning the Tenth Step of Humility

[59]The tenth step of humility is that a monk is not lighthearted, being ready and prompt to laughter, for it is written, "The fool raises his voice in laughter."

VII.11. Concerning the Eleventh Step of Humility

[60]The eleventh step of humility is that when a monk speaks, he does so gently and without laughter, humbly and with gravity, with few words and reasonably. And his voice is not overly loud, [61]as it is written: "The wise man is revealed by his few words."

---

[89] "what . . . superiors": expanding *RB 1980* 7.55, "quod communis monasterii regula vel maiorum cohortantur exempla" ("what is endorsed by the common rule of the monastery and the example set by his superiors").

VII.12. Concerning the Twelfth Step of Humility

[62]The twelfth step of humility is that a monk is humble within his heart—and not this only, but he should also appear that way outwardly in the humility of his body to all those who see him at any task, [63]whether at work,[90] in the oratory, in the monastery, in the garden, on a journey, or in the field. And whether he sits, stands, or walks, he should bend his head down and direct his vision toward the earth. [64]He should reckon himself guilty at every hour on account of his sins and must likewise consider himself already at the fearful Judgment of God, [65]ever saying in his thoughts what the sinful man said with his eyes directed toward the earth—<he whom the holy gospel praises for knowing himself to be guilty and corrupt and who, lamenting>, called out, *Lord, I am not worthy, being such a sinner, to lift my eyes to heaven.** [66]Again, let us say with the prophet, *I am everywhere bowed down and humbled.**

*Luke 18:13

*Ps 37 [38]:7-9; Ps 118 [119]:107

[67]Therefore, once the monk ascends all these steps of humility, he immediately comes to the *true love* of God. Through that love he will be *separated from the fear* of hell's punishments.[91]* [68]Through that love he will begin to observe naturally and as if by custom what before he could not observe without great fear. He observes the customary good of a holy life [69]not because of a fear of hell's punishments but of a singular

*1 John 4:18

---

[90] "at work": translating the *receptus* and *interpolatus* reading "in opera" instead of *RB 1980* 7.63, "in opere dei" ("at the Work of God").

[91] "Through . . . punishments": expanding *RB 1980* 7.67, "*ad caritatem* Dei . . . illam quae *perfecta foris mittit timorem*" ("that *perfect love* of God which *casts out fear*"). "true love": here I translate OE *soþ lufu*—which itself translates Lat "caritas"—as "true love," since "charity of God" is simply not idiomatic in modern English; cf. n. 39 above.

love of God and a desire for holy virtues.[92] [70]At a certain time, the Lord will by the Holy Spirit show all this in his laborer, now cleansed of all vices and sins.

VIII. Concerning the Divine Services at Night

[1]In the winter, that is, from the first of the month called November until Easter, we should arise at the eighth hour of the night. [2]In this way the monks sleep a little more than half the night, the day's food may be digested during their nightly rest, <the heat of their food may be reduced, and the stomach lightened, that each may more easily observe Vigils>.[93] [3]What is left of the night after Vigils should be employed <not in sleep but> in psalmody and instruction in the spiritual craft.[94]

[4]From Easter until the first of November (mentioned above), the beginning of Vigils should be so measured that a little space of time between Vigils and Lauds allows a chance to take care of nature's needs to whoever needs to. And Lauds should begin at once at the onset of daybreak. <The hour's song is thus to begin at that time both in winter and summer.>

[92] "He . . . virtues": expanding *RB 1980* 7.69, "non iam timore gehennae, sed amore Christi et consuetudine ipsa bona et delectatione virtutum" ("no longer out of fear of hell, but out of love for Christ, good habit and delight in virtue").

[93] "the heat . . . Vigils": cf. Smaragdus, Expositio 8.2 (194; Comm 312), "id est iam cibo ab stomachi olla cocto et in ventriculum deducto, somnoque surgant exhalato" ("that is, they may rise, their food having already been cooked by the pot which is the stomach and brought down into the belly and breathed out by sleep").

[94] "not in sleep": Æthelwold may take this clarification from Smaragdus, Expositio 8.3 (195; Comm 313), "Non hic dormire, sicut quidam volunt beatus Benedictus sed vigilare jubet" ("Blessed Benedict does not here bid us to sleep, as some would have it, but to watch").

IX. How Many Psalms Should Be Sung at the Night Offices

¹In the winter, Vigils begins like this: first, say the verse, *Deus in adiutorium meum intende.*⁹⁵* Then three times say, *Domine labia mea aperies.* ²After this, the psalm text, *Domine quid multiplicati sunt.*⁹⁶* ³Then the invitatory with the psalm *Venite exultemus domino.*⁹⁷* ⁴After this a hymn appropriate to the hour is sung.⁹⁸ Then six psalms with <three> refrains.

⁵After this, the abbot gives the blessing.⁹⁹ Someone reads three lections and three responsories,¹⁰⁰ during which all the brothers sit. ⁶After the third responsory the cantor sings the *Gloria patri,* ⁷and all the brothers

*Ps 69 [70]:2

*Ps 3:1
*Ps 94 [95]:1

---

⁹⁵ Earlier manuscripts of RB begin with the verse *"Domine labia mea aperies"* repeated thrice; later manuscripts include the insertion of this verse, which Benedict places at the beginning of the day hours (see chap. XVII below); cf. citations in J. B. L. Tolhurst, ed., *Introduction to the English Monastic Breviaries* (1942; Woodbridge: Boydell Press, 1993), 8 n. 1.

⁹⁶ *"Domine quid multiplicati sunt"*: replacing *RB 1980* 9.2, "tertius psalmus" ("psalm 3") and omitting "et gloria" ("with 'Glory be to the Father'"). Because Æthelwold replaces the psalms' numbers with their opening words in Latin, I retain the Latin as a cue that these are used as titles even for his vernacular audience. Presumably the Latin tags would be helpful to those reading the Old English Rule to link the text's vernacular instructions to the actual experience of hearing the Latin psalmody in liturgical and/or paraliturgical celebration.

⁹⁷ *"Venite exultemus domino"*: replacing *RB 1980* 9.3, "psalmum nonagesimum quartum cum antiphona, aut certe decantandum" ("Psalm 94 with a refrain, or at least chanted").

⁹⁸ "a hymn . . . sung": replacing *RB 1980* 9.4, "Inde sequatur ambrosianum" ("an Ambrosian hymn").

⁹⁹ "After . . . blessing": omitting *RB 1980* 9.5, "dicto versu" ("a versicle is said").

¹⁰⁰ "Someone . . . responsories": omitting the *receptus* and *purus* reading "canantur/cantentur" ("are sung") present in *RB 1980* 9.5.

arise in honor of the Holy Trinity.[101] [8]At Vigils one reads the books of divine teaching, of both the Old Testament and the New, and also holy expositions from the work of celebrated and catholic fathers.[102]

[9]After these three readings and responsories are finished, another six psalms are sung with *Alleluia*. [10]After this follows a reading from the teaching of the apostle said by memory without a book,[103] then a versicle, and then a prayer of supplication—that is, *Kyrieleison*—[11]and and so the night's Vigils are concluded.

X. How the Night Office Is Observed in Summer

[1]From Easter until the first of November, the same practice and same number of psalms as we spoke of above are observed at Vigils, [2]except that the lector does not read from the book because of the shortness of the nights in summer. Rather than those three readings, a single reading from the Old Testament is read by memory without a book,[104] and a very short responsory follows. [3]In everything else, let it be observed in the summer as in winter, so that there are never any fewer psalms sung at Vigils than twelve, not counting *Domine quid multiplicati sunt* and *Uenite exultemus Domino*.

---

[101] Omitting the *receptus* and *purus* reading "duo responsaria sine gloria dicantur" ("'Glory be to the Father' is not sung after the first two responsories"), present in *RB 1980* 9.6.

[102] Omitting *RB 1980* 9.8, "orthodoxis" ("orthodox").

[103] "from . . . book": expansion of RB 9.10, "ex corde recitanda" ("recited by heart").

[104] "without a book": expansion of RB 10.2, "memoriter dicatur" ("said by memory" [my translation]).

XI. How the <Nightly> Vigils Are Observed on Sundays

[1]On Sunday, one must rise earlier [than on other days] for Vigils. [2]In these Vigils one must observe the same number we spoke of above, that is, the twelve psalms. One first sings six psalms with the versicle at the end.[105] After this, all present sit in their proper order, and one reads four readings with four responsories. [3]At the fourth responsory, when the *Gloria Patri* is sung, they all arise in reverence.

[4]After this, they sing the other six psalms with three antiphons and the versicle, [5]following this with four more readings with their responsories following the same order that we explained before. [6]After this, there are three canticles from the books of the prophets, chosen by the abbot and said with *Alleluias*. [7]After a versicle and a blessing given by the abbot, four readings from the New Testament are read following the same order that we explained above. [8]After the *Gloria* following the fourth responsory, the abbot begins the hymn *Te deum laudamus*. [9]When that is finished, the abbot reads the gospel with reverence and divine fear as all present stand. [10]At the end of the gospel, everyone responds *Amen*, after which the abbot begins the *Te decet laus*. After a final blessing, Lauds begin.

[11]This order for Sunday Vigils should be observed in the same manner every time, in both the summer and winter, [12]unless it happen by chance that someone rise later than is fitting and the responsories be left out and the readings shortened. [13]Such negligence should not occur: eagerly guard against such a thing happening. But if it does, let the one who has caused such a thing through his negligence make satisfaction to God in the oratory.

---

[105] "versicle at the end": here Æthelwold retains the versicle ("versu," *RB 1980* 11.2) though he had left it out in his translation of *RB 1980* 9.5.

XII. How Lauds Are Observed on Feast Days

[1]At Lauds on Sunday, one first sings Psalm 66—
<that is, *Deus misereatur nostri*>.[106] [2]After this, Psalm
50—<that is, *Miserere mei deus*>—follows with *Allelu-
lia*. [3]After this comes Psalm 117—<that is, *Confitemini
domino*>—and then Psalm 62—<that is, *Deus, deus
meus, ad te de luce*>. [4]After these come <the Canticle of
the Three Young Men—that is>, the *Benedicite*—and
then *laudes*—<that is, *Laudate dominum de celis*>. After
these a reading from the Apocalypse is said by memory without a book, [and then] a responsory, hymn,
versicle, the gospel Canticle—<that is, *Benedictus dominus deus Israhel*>—and the litany—<that is, *Kyrieleison—Pater noster*, and a collect>: and so Lauds is
completed.[107]

XIII. How They Are Observed on Ordinary Days

[1]On ordinary days, the celebration of Lauds is observed in the following way. [2]Psalm 66—<that is, *Deus
misereatur nostri*>—is said without antiphon and is
somewhat lengthened as on Sunday so that all the
members of the monastery may be gathered together
by the beginning of Psalm 50—<that is, *Miserere mei*

---

[106] The names of psalms and canticles in chapters XII and XIII
are additions.

[107] "by memory . . . book": expansion of *RB 1980* 12.4, "ex
corde" ("by heart"). Though the *Pater noster* and collect are not
explicitly prescribed in chapter twelve of RB, Benedict does
note that neither Lauds nor Vespers should end without the
superior's recitation aloud of the Lord's Prayer (see chapter XIII
below). Additionally, the use of the Lord's Prayer, "preces" (a
"series of psalm verses sung as versicle and response between
officiant and choir"), and the collect following the canticle and
litany varied (see John Harper, *The Forms and Orders of the Western Liturgy from the Tenth to the Eighteenth Century* [Oxford: Clarendon Press, 1991], 84, chap. eight).

deus>—which is said with an antiphon. ³After these, according to custom, a further two psalms are said: ⁴on the second day Psalms 5 and 35—<that is, *Uerba mea* and *Dixit iniustus>*; ⁵on the third day Psalms 42 and 56—<that is, *Judica me deus* and *Miserere mei deus, miserere mei>*; ⁶on the fourth day Psalms 63 and 64—<that is, *Exaudi deus orationem meam cum tribulor* and *Te decet ymnus deus>*; ⁷on the fifth day Psalms 87 and 89—<that is, *Domine deus salutis mee* and *Domine refugium>*; ⁸on the sixth day Psalms 75 and 91—<that is, *Notus in Judea deus* and *Bonum est confiteri domino>*; ⁹on the seventh day Psalm 142—<that is, *Domine exaudi orationem meam auribus percipe>*—and the Canticle from Deuteronomy—<that is, *Adtende celum>*—which is divided and accompanied by two *Glorias*. ¹⁰On the other days of the week a canticle—<that is, a song of praise>—proper to the day is sung, according to the practice of the Roman church:[108] on Monday, <*Confitebor>**; on Tuesday, <*Ego dixi>*†; on Wednesday, <*Exultauit>*#; on Thursday, <*Cantemus>*‡; on Friday, <*Domine audiui>*∞; on Saturday, <*Adtende celum>*.[109]◊ ¹¹After this on each day, *laudes*—<that is, *Laudate dominum de celis>*—are said with a reading from the teaching of

*Isa 12:1-6
†Isa 38:10-20
#1 Sam 2:1-10
‡Exod 15:1-19
∞Hab 3:1-19
◊Deut 32:1-21
and 22-43

---

[108] "that . . . sung": translating *RB 1980* 13.10, "canticum unumquemque die suo ex prophetis" ("a Canticle from the Prophets is said").

[109] "On Monday . . . celum": Æthelwold supplies the names of the canticles to be sung at Lauds, which are not found in RB. Though individual monasteries did not necessarily follow precisely the same usage for the canticles, those listed here by Æthelwold reflect "a consensus from English medieval houses" based on the researches of J. B. L. Tolhurst in his *The Monastic Breviary of Hyde Abbey*, 6 vols. (London: Henry Bradshaw Society, 1932), 42, as cited in Harper, *Forms and Orders*, 256–57. Æthelwold's list matches the canticles copied and glossed in the Anglo-Saxon Vespasian Psalter, a *Romanum* psalter copied in the eighth century, for which see *The Vespasian Psalter*, ed Sherman M. Kuhn (Ann Arbor: The University of Michigan Press, 1965), 147–55.

the apostle by memory, without a book.[110] Then a responsory, a hymn, a versicle, the Gospel canticle—<that is, *Benedictus*>—and the litany: and so Lauds are completed.

[12]Assuredly, neither Lauds nor Vespers should be ended without the Lord's Prayer—<that is, the *Pater noster*>. But the superior should sing that whole prayer in a loud voice for all to hear. [13]In this way, everyone may know for himself whether he holds anything discordant or deceitful in his thoughts and so may cleanse himself from every hateful vice by means of what he hears in this prayer:[111] *Dimitte nobis debita nostra, sicut et nos dimittimus debitoribus nostris**— <that is, in our language, *Lord, forgive us our sins, just as we forgive those who sin against us*>.[112] [14]At the other hours, only the ending is said aloud <by the priest>, that all the others may respond, *Sed libera nos a malo.*

*Matt 6:12

XIV. How the <Nightly> Vigils Are Observed on Feast Days

[1]On the feasts of <God's> saints, and on all feast days <that occur in the year's cycle>, all the services should be done according to the number and the order observed on Sunday—[2]though the psalms, antiphons, responsories, and readings appropriate to the feast day are sung. In everything else, the same number is to be observed as occurs on Sundays.

[110] "by . . . book": expansion of *RB 1980* 13.11, "memoriter recitanda" ("recited by memory").

[111] "In . . . thoughts": freely translating *RB 1980* 13.12, "propter scandalorum spinas quae oriri solent" ("because thorns of contention are likely to spring up").

[112] "that . . . *us*": Here Æthelwold explicitly notes the Latin/Old English distinction with which he is working.

XV. Concerning the Times *Alleluia* Should Be Sung

¹From Easter until Pentecost, *Alleluia* is said without interruption with both the psalms and the responsories. ²From Pentecost until the beginning of Lent, *Alleluia* is said every night with the last six psalms. ³Except during Lent, Vigils, Lauds, Prime, Terce, Sext, and None are sung with *Alleluia* every Sunday. Vespers is said with an antiphon. ⁴Responsories are never sung with *Alleluia*, except from Easter until Pentecost.

XVI. How the Divine Office Should Be Performed during the Day

¹Let us do as the prophet says, *Seven times a day I have praised you, Lord, and spoken your praise.*¹¹³* ²We fulfill this sevenfold reckoning if we fulfill the ministration of our service in Lauds, Prime, Terce, Sext, Vespers, and Compline. ³Concerning these hours the prophet said,¹¹⁴ *Seven times a day I have praised you, Lord.** ⁴The same prophet says concerning Vigils, *At midnight I arose, Lord, to praise you.** ⁵Therefore, let us *praise* our Creator *for the judgments of* his *righteousness* at these times—that is, at Lauds, Prime, Terce, Sext, None, Vespers, Compline.* And *at night let us arise and praise the Lord.*¹¹⁵*

*Ps 118 [119]:164

*Ps 118 [119]:164
*Ps 118 [119]:62

*Ps 118 [119]:164
*Ps 118 [119]:62

---

¹¹³ "Let . . . *praise*": Æthelwold here turns the observation of *RB 1980* 16.1 into an exhortation, using the common homiletic exhortation OE *Uton* ("Let us").

¹¹⁴ "hours": translating the *receptus* and *interpolatus* reading "de his horis" ("concerning these hours") instead of *RB 1980* 16.3, "de his diurnis horis" ("concerning these hours during the day").

¹¹⁵ "*at night . . . Lord*": though the text of the psalm is altered here, the change is found in *RB 1980*, which Æthelwold follows.

XVII. How Many Psalms Should Be Said at the Seven Hours[116]

¹Now we have arranged the order of the psalmody for Vigils and Lauds. Let us presently consider the other hours.

²At Prime three psalms are sung, each followed by the *Gloria*. ³Before one begins the psalms, a hymn appropriate to the hour is sung after the versicle *Deus in adiutorium meum intende.** ⁴After these three psalms, a reading is said with a versicle and the *Kyrrieleison*. It is finished with prayers.[117]

*Ps 69 [70]:2

⁵At Terce, Sext, and None, the same order of prayer is celebrated: the versicle, a hymn appropriate to the hour, three psalms, a reading, a versicle, the *Kyrrieleison*, and finish with prayers. ⁶If the community is large, they are sung with antiphons; if the community is small, they are sung plainly without music.[118]

⁷The praise at Vespers is limited to four psalms with their antiphons. ⁸After these four psalms, a reading is recited, and then a responsory, hymn, versicle, gospel canticle—<that is, *Magnificat*>—the litany—<that is, *Kyrrieleison*>—and the Lord's Prayer—<that is, *Pater noster*>. It is finished with prayers.[119]

---

[116] "should be said": translating the *receptus* reading "dicendi sunt" instead of *RB 1980* 17, "canendi sunt" ("to be sung").

[117] "It . . . prayers": translating *RB 1980* 17.4, "et missas" ("and the dismissal").

[118] "they are sung plainly . . . music": translating *RB 1980* 17.6, "in directum psallantur." Here it is difficult to know whether Æthelwold understood the liturgical terminology found throughout RB in the same way modern scholars do. Following Vogüé, Fry translates the Latin as "the psalms are said without refrain," taking *RB 1980*'s "antiphona" to mean a "refrain" recited by the community in response to a soloist's chanting of a psalm's verses (see Fry, 402–3). Whether or not this accords with Benedict's original milieu, it is unclear whether Æthelwold did or could have understood these terms in the same way.

[119] "It . . . prayers": translating *RB 1980* 17.8, "missae" ("the dismissal").

[9]Compline is limited to three psalms, which are sung plainly without antiphons. [10]After these are hymns appropriate to the hour, a reading, versicle, and *Kyrrieleison*, and it is finished with prayers.[120]

XVIII. The Order of the Psalms to Be Said[121]

[1]The day hours always begin with the versicle[122] *Deus in adiutorium meum intende,** the *Gloria patri*, and a hymn appropriate to the hour.

*Ps 69 [70]:2

[2]Then there are four sections—<that is, four different divisions>—of Psalm 118—<that is, *Beati immaculati* or *legem pone*>.[123] [3]At the other hours—that is, at Terce, Sext, and None—three sections from the same psalm are sung. At Terce: from *legem pone** to *portio mea*#; from *portio mea* to *defecit*‡; from *defecit* to *lucerne*◊.

*v. 33
#v. 57
‡v. 81
◊v. 105

[4]On Monday three psalms are sung at Prime: the first, the second, and the sixth—<that is, *Beatus uir, Quare fremuerunt gentes*, and *Domine, ne in furore tuo*>. [5]On the other days of the week, three psalms are sung through Psalm 19. Psalms 9 and 17—<that is, *Confitebor* and *Diligam te*>—are divided in two <with the *Gloria*>. [6]Thus they are arranged so that Vigils on Sunday begins with Psalm 20—<that is, *Domine, in uirtute tua*>.

[7]On Monday at Terce, Sext, and None, three sections each of the remaining nine sections of Psalm 118 are sung. [8]Psalm 118 is thus finished in two days, that is,

---

[120] "it . . . prayers": translating *RB 1980* 17.10, "et benedictione missae" ("a blessing and the dismissal").

[121] "psalms": translating the *receptus* reading *psalmi* instead of *RB 1980* 18, "ipsi psalmi" ("these psalms" [my translation]).

[122] "The day hours always begin": translating the *receptus* and *interpolatus* reading "semper diurnis horis" ("always at the day hours") instead of *RB 1980* 18.1, "in primis" ("At the beginnings" [my translation])

[123] Omitting "prima hora dominica" ("on Sunday at Prime") from the beginning of *RB 1980* 18.2.

on Sunday and Monday. [9]On Tuesday at Terce, Sext, and None three psalms each are sung from the nine psalms between 119 and 127. [10]The same psalms are repeated daily at these hours throughout the week until Sunday. The hymns, capitular readings, versicles, and litanies are observed in the same manner of which we spoke above. [11]And so Sunday always begins again with Psalm 118—<that is, *Beati immaculati*>.

[12]Vespers has four psalms each day. [13]The psalms begin with Psalm 109 and go through 147—<that is, from *Dixit dominus* through *Laudate dominum de celis*>—[14]except those which are already set apart for other hours. These include Psalms 117 through 127—<that is, from *Beati immaculati* through *Sepe expugnauerunt me*>[124]—as well as Psalms 133 and 142—<that is, *Ecce nunc* and *Domine exaudi*>. [15]All the others are sung at Evensong.[125] [16]Since this reckoning of the psalms results in too few, the three longest psalms must be divided in two <with the *Gloria*>. These are Psalms 138, 143, and 144—<that is, *Domine probasti me*, *Benedictus*, and *Exaltabo te domine*>. [17]Because Psalm 116 is too short, it must be combined with Psalm 115 <and the two sung as one psalm>. [18]This is the order of the psalms at Vespers. The rest is fulfilled as I arranged it above: that is, the reading, responsory, hymn, versicle, and canticle—<that is, the *Magnificat*>.

---

[124] "*Beati immaculati*": this appears to be an error on Æthelwold's part, since "Psalm . . . 117" translates *RB 1980* 18.14 ("centesimo septimo decimo") correctly, but he gives the Latin incipit (*Beati immaculati*) for Psalm 118 [119] (identified correctly in the preceding paragraph) rather than 117 [118], which would be *Confitemini Domino*.

[125] "Even-song": here Æthelwold varies his usual OE word for *vespers* (*æfensang*), using OE *æfendreame* (which I translate with the now-less-common *Evensong*), though *RB 1980* does not vary its use of Lat "vespera."

¹⁹At Compline, one repeats the same psalms each night: Psalms 4, 90, and 133—<that is, *Cum inuocarem te*, *Qui habitat*, and *Ecce nunc*>.

Thus the daily order of the psalmody is arranged. ²⁰All the other psalms that remain are divided evenly between the seven Vigils of the week. ²¹The longer psalms are divided in two with a *Gloria*, so that twelve psalms are sung at Vigils each night.

²²Above all, we exhort anyone who is unsatisfied with this arrangement and order of the psalmody to arrange and order it in a manner that seems better to him—²³though he must take care that all one hundred and fifty psalms of the psalter are divided and sung <at the hours> each week.¹²⁶ ²⁴For monks are wholly negligent in their service of obedience if they sing less than the whole psalter and the customary canticles each week. ²⁵We have read that our venerable fathers strenuously fulfilled this duty in a single day.¹²⁷ We in our idleness and weakness should accomplish the same in an entire week!

XIX. Concerning the Discipline of Psalmody

¹We believe that God's presence and sight are everywhere, and that *his eyes watch both the good and the evil*.¹²⁸* ²But without a doubt we should believe this most firmly when we are at the Work of God. *Prov 15:3

³Therefore, we must always be mindful of what the prophet says: *Serve your Lord with fear*.* ⁴And again, *Ps 2:11
Sing wisely.* ⁵And, *In the sight of the angels I will sing to* *Ps 46 [47]:8

---

¹²⁶ Omitting RB 18.23, "et dominico die semper a caput reprehendatur ad vigilias" ("and that the series begins anew each Sunday at Vigils").

¹²⁷ "venerable": translating *RB 1980* 18.25, "sanctos" ("holy") as OE *ealdan*.

¹²⁸ Omitting the *receptus* and *interpolatus* reading "in omni loco," which is present in *RB 1980* 19.1.

*you.** [6]Therefore, let us consider how we conduct ourselves in the sight of God and his angels. [7]And let us
so stand at the psalmody that our minds accord with
the words of our mouth.[129]

XX. Concerning Reverence in Prayer

[1]If we wish to make known one of our needs to a
wealthy person, we do not presume to do so without
great humility. [2]How much more then should we entreat the Lord of all creatures with all humility, <sub-
mission>, and sincerity of spirit?[130] [3]We must know
that we are not heard because of the great number of
our prayers, but, rather, our prayers are received because of the purity of our hearts and our tears of compunction. [4]Therefore, prayer should be short and pure,
unless someone is urged by divine compunction to
lengthen his prayer.[131] [5]But in the community's as-
sembly, prayer should be short. At the designated
signal from the superior, all should rise together.

XXI. What Kind of Men the Deans of the Monastery Must Be[132]

[1]If the community is large, some of the brothers
known for their good sense and holy life should be

---

[129] "words of our mouth": translating *RB 1980* 19.7, "voci nos-
trae" ("our voices").

[130] "sincerity of spirit": translating *RB 1980* 20.2, "puritatis
devotione" ("sincerity of devotion").

[131] "Therefore . . . his prayer": freely translating *RB 1980* 20.4,
"nisi forte ex affectu inspirationis divinae gratiae protendatur"
("unless perhaps it is prolonged under the inspiration of divine
grace").

[132] "What . . . Be": translating the *receptus* reading "Decani
monasterii quales debeant esse" instead of *RB 1980* 21, "De
decanis monasterii" ("The deans of the monastery").

chosen and made deans.[133] [2]They will be solicitous and caring in their positions of authority, performing every task according to God's commands and their abbot's behest. [3]The superiors selected should be men with whom the abbot can share his burden. [4]They should not be chosen according to rank, but for the merits of their lives and their wise teaching.

[5]If by chance one of the deans becomes puffed up on account of the trust accorded him for his position of authority and exalts himself in pride[134] and he is found to be in sin, let him be corrected once, twice, and a third time. If he does not improve and rectify himself, he is to be cast out from his position of authority [6]and another who is worthy set in his place. [7]We prescribe and teach the same regarding the prior.

XXII. The Monks' Sleeping Arrangements

[1]The monks are to sleep alone in separate beds. [2]They receive bedding appropriate to the monastic life and as their abbot directs.

[3]If it is possible, they should all sleep in the same building. If their number is so great that they cannot, let them sleep together in one place in tens or twenties with the superiors who care for them. [4]A light should be kept burning continually in the room until morning light.

[5]They sleep clothed and girded but should not have their knives at their sides lest they hurt themselves in their sleep. [6]This way they will always be prepared to arise at the designated signal without delay. Each will

---

[133] "good sense": translating *RB 1980* 21.1, "boni testimonii" ("good repute"). One manuscript has OE *gewitnes*, which is a literal translation of Lat *testimonium* ("witness"), but this OE word is not attested as possessing the connotation of "reputation," as the Lukan reference (Acts 6:3) in *RB 1980* does.

[134] "becomes . . . pride": translating *RB 1980* 21.5, "inflatus superbia repertus" ("is found to be puffed up with any pride").

quickly go before the others and hasten to the Work
of God—though with great gravity and modesty. [7]The
young should not lie next to one another, but older
monks should lie mixed in with the young. [8]When
they arise for the Work of God, each should exhort the
others so that the sleepy will have no excuse.[135]

XXIII. Concerning the Remedy of Faults[136]

[1]If any brother is found to be arrogant or disobedient or proud, or if he grumbles or in any way acts
against the holy rule and despises the commands of
his elders, [2]he should be exhorted secretly with words
twice <or thrice> in accord with God's command.* [3]If
he does not improve nor correct himself, he must be
publicly rebuked before everyone. [4]If then he still will
not correct himself, and if he understands how serious
a punishment it is, let him undergo excommunication.
[5]If he is still contrary, he should suffer bodily pain <by
means of the rod>.[137]

*Matt 18:15-16

XXIV. The Measure Observed in the Remedy[138]

[1]The measure of excommunication or discipline
given must be increased according to the measure of

[135] "so . . . excuse": freely translating *RB 1980* 22.8, "propter
somnulentorum excusationes" ("for the sleepy like to make
excuses").

[136] "the remedy": translating *RB 1980* 23, "Excommunicatione"
("Excommunication") as OE *Bot* ("Remedy").

[137] "contrary": translating *RB 1980* 23.5, "improbus." While
Fry notes (Fry n. to 2.28) that the Lat *improbus* ("evil") can have
a variety of connotations and so translates *RB 1980* 23.5, "improbus" as "lacks understanding," based on the contrast with
RB 1980 23.4, "intellegit" ("understands"), Æthelwold clearly
did not agree.

[138] "the Remedy": see n. to title of chapter XXIII.

one's faults. ²Determining the severity of faults lies in the abbot's judgment.

³Nevertheless, if a brother is found guilty of less severe faults, let him be kept apart from fellowship at table. ⁴This is the degree of punishment observed for those who are kept from the fellowship at meal times: he is not to lead a psalm or a refrain or recite a reading until he has done full penance.[139] ⁵He will take his meals alone after the brothers have taken theirs. ⁶Such is what I say: if the brothers eat at midday, let him eat at mid-afternoon; if they eat at midafternoon, he will eat in the evening. ⁷This will continue until he obtains forgiveness from God by means of a proper penance.[140]

XXV. Concerning Serious Faults

¹A brother who is injured by the weight of grievous faults and seized by serious sins is to be kept apart from sharing the common table as well as from entering the holy church.[141] ²No brother should associate with him at all: neither in speech nor in any other kind of companionship. ³He must continue in his assigned work with repentance and grievous sorrow, considering that fearful saying of the apostle concerning such

---

[139] "full penance": translating *RB 1980* 24.4, "ad satisfactionem" as OE *dædbot*, which has also translated Lat *paenitencia*.

[140] "until . . . penance": translating freely *RB 1980* 24.7, "usque dum satisfactione congrua veniam consequatur" ("until by proper satisfaction he gains pardon"). Æthelwold may have borrowed this interpretation from Smaragdus, Expositio 24.7 (222; Comm 353), "Congrua dicitur satisfactio, quando secundum modum culpae agitur poenitudo" ("Satisfaction is said to be fitting when penance is done according to the measure of fault").

[141] "church": translating *RB 1980* 25.1, "oratorio," as OE *cyrice* ("church"), while Æthelwold translates the same Lat word *oloc* where as OE *ȝebedhus* ("oratory") (e.g., in chapter LII).

guilty parties: **⁴Such a man is handed over to the devil for the destruction of his flesh, so that his spirit may be saved in God's judgment.**¹⁴²* **⁵**He receives his meals alone, in an amount and at a time the abbot considers appropriate for him. **⁶**He should not be blessed by anyone he meets, nor should the food given to him be blessed.

*1 Cor 5:5

XXVI. Concerning Those Who Associate with the Penitent without the Abbot's Permission

¹If a brother presumes to associate with the excommunicated without the abbot's permission in any way, to speak with him or send him a message through another, **²**he must be excommunicated in a similar way and make amends <in similar misery>.

XXVII. How the Abbot Must Be Concerned for the Excommunicated

¹The abbot must have care and concern for the guilty brothers, because *the healthy have no need of a physician or medicine, but the sick.*¹⁴³* **²**Therefore he must employ in his care [for the brothers] a skilled physician's every means. [The abbot] must secretly send in wise and steadfast elders, **³**that they may exhort the wavering and doubtful brother to penitence and his

*Matt 9:12

---

¹⁴² "*Such . . . judgment*": translating *RB 1980* 25.4, "*traditum eiusmodi hominem in interitum carnis, ut spiritus salvus sit in die Domini*" ("*Such a man is handed over for the destruction of his flesh that his spirit may be saved on the day of the Lord*"). "the devil": translating the *receptus* and *interpolatus* reading "satanae" ("Satan" or "the devil")—following the Vulgate, which *RB 1980* 25.4 omits.

¹⁴³ "*the healthy . . . the sick*": translating *RB 1980* 27.1, "*non est opus sanis medicus sed male habentibus*" ("*it is not the healthy who need a physician, but the sick*").

proper duty as well as *console* him *lest he be swallowed up in perdition in his great sorrow.*[144]* [4]*Let love for the sinning brother be confirmed* and made firm, and let all the brothers pray for him.[145]*

[5]It is of the greatest import that the abbot take great care, striving with all his wisdom, not to lose any of the sheep from the flock that has been entrusted to him. [6]He should know that he has taken up the care of unhealthy souls as a just physician, not tyranny over those who are healthy. [7]He should fear as well the threat that comes from the Lord through his prophet, saying, *What you saw was fat you chose for yourselves, and what was weak you cast aside.** [8]But the abbot should imitate the example of the honorable and merciful Shepherd who left the ninety-nine sheep upon the mountain, eagerly looking for and finding the one that had strayed and erred.[146] [9]He had such pity on that sheep's weakness that *he laid it upon his shoulders* and bore it back to the flock.[147]*

*2 Cor 2:7

*2 Cor 2:8

*Ezek 34:3-4

*Luke 15:5

XXVIII. Concerning Those Who Are Often Reproved and Will Not Amend

[1]If a brother has been often and explicitly reproved for any sin, or if he will not amend or put right his behavior even after being excommunicated, let him be reproved with a harsher punishment. That is, let

---

[144] "[The abbot] . . . sorrow": loosely translating *RB 1980* 27.2-3. "*console . . . sorrow*": translating *RB 1980* 27.3, "*consolentur eum ne abundantiori tristitia absorbeatur*" ("*console* him *lest he be overwhelmed by excessive sorrow*").

[145] Omitting *RB 1980* 27.4, "sed, sicut ait item apostolus" ("Rather, as the apostle also says").

[146] "honorable and merciful": translating *RB 1980* 27.8, "boni" ("good"). "the one": translating the *receptus* reading "unam" instead of *RB 1980* 27.8, "unam ovem" ("the one sheep").

[147] "shoulders": omitting *RB 1980* 27.9, "sacris" ("sacred").

him feel the punishment of the rod. ²If he will not correct himself [after punishment with] the rod, but, remaining in his pride, will even in his arrogance defend his evil deeds <with lies>, the abbot must act just like a wise physician.¹⁴⁸ ³If he has provided poultices and the unguents of divine admonitions and the medicine of the Holy Scriptures and finally applied the cauterizing of excommunication and the punishment of the rod, ⁴and he perceives that all his solicitude and wisdom achieve nothing, then let him provide the greatest [remedy]: his own prayers and those of his brothers, ⁵that the Lord, who can do all things and will do all things, may heal the weak and sinful brother. ⁶If he is not healed through those prayers, then the abbot must employ the knife, cutting out the disease with iron and removing it from the holy brothers, according to the admonition of the apostle, who says, *Expel the evil one from your midst,** ⁷and again, *If the unbeliever departs, let him depart,** ⁸lest one diseased sheep pollute the flock.

*1 Cor 5:13
*1 Cor 7:15

XXIX. Concerning Whether Those Who Leave Should Be Received Again

¹If a brother who leaves the monastery or is expelled on account of his own sins or vices desires to return, he must first promise to make amends <and abstain from all those vices on account of which he was expelled>.¹⁴⁹ ²He should be received in last place, so that he might prove thereby whether he has returned in humility. ³If he leaves again <on account of his vices—or is expelled>—he should still be received back the second and third times. After this he must

---

¹⁴⁸ Omitting *RB 1980* 28.2, "quod absit" ("which God forbid").
¹⁴⁹ "and . . . expelled": Æthelwold appears particularly concerned to tighten up the stipulations regarding expulsion from and reentry to the monastery.

understand that he will be denied any admittance and he may never again return to the monastery.

XXX. Concerning the Punishment of Boys

[1]Each age and level of understanding should receive its appropriate punishments. [2]Therefore, when young boys, hardy youths, or those who cannot understand properly how great and serious the punishment of excommunication is [3]are guilty of misdeeds, one should punish them with severe fasts or subdue them with harsh strokes so that they might be healed.

XXXI. Concerning the Monastery's Cellarer

[1]As cellarer of the monastery, let there be chosen from the community a person who is wise, mature in conduct, temperate, not an overeater, not excitable, not offensive, not ostentatious, [2]but one who fears God.[150] Let him be as a father to the whole community. [3]He will take care of everything [4]but will do nothing except at the abbot's behest. [5]Let him keep to what he is commanded.

[6]He should not offend his brothers. [7]If a brother asks something unreasonable of him, [the cellarer] should not offend him by despising the brother, but reasonably refuse the improper request with humility. [8]Let him ever guard his own thoughts, <so that he may serve with a sound mind>.[151] And let him be mindful of that saying of the apostle: *He who serves well secures a good standing for himself.** [9]With all solicitude, he must

*1 Tim 3:13

---

[150] "wise . . . ostentatious": translating *RB 1980* 31.1, "sapiens, maturis moribus, sobrius, non multum edax, non elatus, non turbulentus, non iniuriosus, non tardus, non prodigus" ("wise, mature in conduct, temperate, not an excessive eater, not proud, excitable, offensive, dilatory or wasteful").

[151] "thoughts": translating *RB 1980* 31.8, "animam" ("soul").

have care and concern for the sick, children, guests, and the poor. He must know without a doubt that he will have to render an account for all of them at God's Judgment. [10]He must look upon all the vessels and goods of the monastery as upon the sacred vessels of the altar. [11]He should permit nothing to suffer neglect. [12]He must not be prone to stinginess <or ostentatious>.[152] He must not squander the monastery's property or waste it, but rather do all things with moderation according to the abbot's behest.

[13]Above all things let him have humility. And if he has nothing to give from the monastery's property, let him give a kind word in reply, [14]for it is written, *A kind word is better than the best gift.** [15]Let him have under his care all that the abbot has entrusted to him. In addition, let him not presume to do what has been forbidden. [16]Let him provide his brothers their food at the proper time without delay or complaint, lest they be offended. Let him be mindful of that divine saying concerning what is earned by him *who offends one of the least who trusts in God.**

[17]If the congregation is large, he should be given aid and help. With [the brothers'] help he may gladly fulfill the service allotted to him with a calm and joyful spirit. [18]Those things that are to be given and requested should be given and requested at the proper times, [19]so that no one is troubled or offended in God's house.

*Sir 18:17

*Matt 18:6

XXXII. Concerning the Tools and Goods of the Monastery

[1]The monastery's goods—its tools, clothing, or any other thing—should be entrusted for oversight to brothers whose lives and good customs the abbot

---

[152] "stinginess": translating *RB 1980* 31.12 "avaritiae" ("greed").

deems distinguished and trustworthy. ²He entrusts to them the items that must be cared for and subsequently returned. ³The abbot always keeps a written account of all these goods. When the brothers take up different work, the abbot will know certainly what he entrusts to them and what he receives back from them.

⁴If someone fails to keep the monastery's items clean or treats them carelessly, let him be reproved. If he will not amend, let him be subjected to a proper punishment.[153]

XXXIII. Concerning How Monks Should Not Own Private Property

¹Above all and most profoundly, this evil practice must be removed and completely uprooted from the monastery: ²no one should presume to give or receive anything except at the abbot's behest. ³Nor may anyone retain a private possession, nothing at all—not a book, a wax tablet, a stylus, or any other thing. ⁴For what can someone keep for his own when he no longer has his own body and spirit within his own power?[154] ⁵He will hope for and desire everything necessary from the father of his monastery, and he will have

---

[153] "proper punishment": translating *RB 1980* 32.5, "disciplinae regulari" ("the discipline of the rule").

[154] "For, . . . spirit": translating *RB 1980* 33.4, "quippe quibus nec corpora sua nec voluntates licet habere in propria voluntate" ("especially since monks may not have the free disposal even of their own bodies and wills"). Here Æthelwold follows Smaragdus, Expositio 33.4 (242–43; Comm 387), "Quid enim proprium habere potest sanctus monachus, qui nec corpus suum nec voluntatem suam in suam reservavit potestatem . . . ?" ("For what can a holy monk have as his own, when he has not reserved his own body or his own will to his own power . . . ?"). "power": translating the *receptus* reading "potestate" instead of *RB 1980* 33.4, "voluntate" ("free disposal").

nothing that the abbot does not provide and permit. ⁶*Everything is common* to them all, just as it is written concerning the apostles' manner of life—<which exemplifies monastic life>—*lest anyone* presume *to possess anything as his own or call anything his own.**

*Acts 4:32

⁷If anyone indulges in this most evil and perverse practice, let him either desist at the admonition of his elders, ⁸or let him be tamed with serious bodily punishment.

XXXIV. Concerning How Monks Should Not Be Treated Alike

¹Everything necessary and licit should be given to them, reflecting that which is written about the apostles' manner of life: *To each it was given as he had need.** ²We do not understand this saying to mean that there should be any favoritism—that is, that consideration should be given to one's greatness—but that consideration should be given to one's need and sickness.¹⁵⁵ ³Those in the community who have fewer and simpler needs should thank God and not be saddened, <though more is done for those who have greater needs>. ⁴Those who have greater needs <on account of some bodily frailty> should be humbled by their weakness, not exalted as if they were shown kindness <because of their merits or rank>. ⁵Thus will all the members be at peace. ⁶Before all else we warn against the appearance of the evil of grumbling for any reason in word or sign. ⁷If someone is found in this vice, let him be tamed with severe punishment.

*Acts 4:35

---

¹⁵⁵ "We . . . sickness": translating *RB 1980* 34.2, "Ubi non dicimus ut personarum—quod absit—acceptio sit, sed infirmitatum consideratio" ("By this we do not imply that there should be favoritism—God forbid—but rather consideration for weaknesses").

XXXV. Concerning the Weekly Servers

[1]The brothers should serve each other. And no one should be excused from kitchen service except for those who are sick or are weighed down by important business <in such a way that they are unable to fulfill this role>.[156] [2]Through this obedience of common service we receive the greatest love from God and from others.[157] [3]Let those who are weak and feeble be given assistance, that they may perform their obedience without distress. [4]Let everyone have assistance and aid according to the size of the community and the conditions and state of the locality. [5]If the community is large, the cellarer should be given a replacement, as should those weighed down by serious and important business. [6]Let everyone else serve one another.[158]

[7]On Saturday the weekly kitchen servers wash the utensils [8]as well as the towels with which [the brothers] wipe their hands and feet. [9]Let both the past week's servers and the coming week's servers wash the feet of all the brothers that day. [10]The utensils for their service should be given back to the cellarer clean and in good condition. [11]The cellarer then gives the same utensils to the servers for the upcoming week. He ought to know both what he receives and what he gives away.[159]

[12]An hour before the common meal, the weekly servers should receive bread and drink privately—

---

[156] "And": translating the *receptus* reading "et" instead of *RB 1980* 35.1, "ut" ("Consequently"). "weighed down by": translating *RB 1980* 35.1, "occupatus fuerit" ("is . . . engaged").

[157] "the . . . others": freely translating *RB 1980* 35.2, "quia exinde maior merces et caritas acquiritur" ("for such service increases reward and fosters love").

[158] Omitting *RB 1980* 35.6, "sub caritate" ("in love").

[159] "what he receives . . . away": translating *RB 1980* 35.11, "dat aut quod recipit" ("what he hands out and what he receives back").

<and this should be before everyone sits down to their food>—[13]so that they may more gladly serve their brothers at mealtime without hardship or great trouble.[160] [14]However, on feast days they do not have their bread and drink until after Mass.

[15]On Sundays immediately following Lauds, the weekly servers—both those who are completing and those beginning their weeks—should bow in the church before the knees of all the brothers and ask for their prayers.[161] [16]When those who have ended their weekly service step down they recite this verse, giving thanks: *Blessed are you, almighty Lord, who have helped and comforted me.** [17]When they say this verse three times, they receive a blessing and step down from their weekly service. The servers for the coming week follow and say, *Come to my assistance, God; Lord, make haste to help me.** [18]The whole community repeats this

*Dan 3:52; Ps 85 [86]:17

*Ps 69 [70]:2

---

[160] "hardship or great trouble": translating *RB 1980* 35.13, "murmuratione et gravi labore" ("grumbling or hardship"). While Æthelwold translates various words in *RB 1980* with words that reflect Modern English "grumbling," here he chooses to translate Lat "murmuratio" ("grumbling") as OE *gedeorf*, the semantic range of which suggests "hardship," "trouble," and "labor," which is closer in literal sense to the second element in *RB 1980* 35.13, "gravi labore"—though he also translates "gravi labore" literally as OE *miclum geswince*.

[161] "should . . . brothers": apparently translating (inaccurately?) *RB 1980* 35.15, "omnibus genibus provolvantur" ("should make a profound bow . . . before all"). Fry notes that the oldest extant manuscript of RB, Oxford, Bodleian Library, Hatton 48, contains the variant reading Lat "omnium" here, which would translate literally (and more explicitly) as Æthelwold's OE *ealra ȝeferena* (35.15 n). While this variant fits Æthelwold's translation, Gretsch, DRB, does not cite this variant, one that belongs to the *interpolatus* recension and is not found in any of the extant *receptus* manuscripts from Anglo-Saxon England. If this is not simply a misinterpretation of the Latin on Æthelwold's part, it could point to a variant in the RB text(s) he was using that does not survive in the extant *receptus* manuscripts.

verse three times, and with a blessing they begin their weekly service.

XXXVI. Concerning the Sick Brothers

¹Care of the sick should be placed above all things, so that they may be served like God himself, ²for he says, *I was sick, and you visited me,** ³and *What you did for one of these least, who are mine, that you did for me.*¹⁶²* ⁴Let the sick know that they are served and obeyed out of honor for God and that they should not trouble the brothers who serve them with excessive demands. ⁶Indeed, the abbot must take the greatest care that they are not neglected.¹⁶³

*Matt 25:36
*Matt 25:40

⁷Let a separate room be established for the sick brothers, and let their care be entrusted to an attendant who is attentive and possesses the love and the fear of God.¹⁶⁴ ⁸The sick may take baths with permission as often as is beneficial. The well and especially the young should be allowed this less frequently and less readily. ⁹The sick and the infirm may be permitted to eat meat to regain their health. But once they have recovered and regained their strength, they should abstain from meat according to the usual custom.

¹⁰The abbot must take the greatest care that the sick are not neglected by the cellarers or their attendants, for he is responsible for what his disciples neglect.

---

¹⁶² *"who are mine"*: translating the *receptus* and *interpolatus* reading "meis," which *RB 1980* 36.3 omits.

¹⁶³ Omitting *RB 1980* 36.5, "qui tamen patienter portandi sunt, quia de talibus copiosior merces acquiritur" ("Still, sick brothers must be patiently borne with, because serving them leads to a greater reward").

¹⁶⁴ "attentive . . . God": translating *RB 1980* 36.7, "timens Deum et diligens ac sollicitus" ("God-fearing, attentive, and concerned").

XXXVII. Concerning the Elderly Monks and Children

¹Although it is human nature to be compassionate to the elderly and the young, nevertheless they should not be left out of the rule, which is the guide for our way of life.¹⁶⁵ ²As their weakness is always evident, they should not be held to the strictness of the rule with regard to their food. ³Compassion should be shown to them, and they should be permitted to eat and drink before the regular hours.

XXXVIII. Concerning the Weekly Reader

¹The brothers' meals at table should not be without reading. Let no one presume to take up the book by chance and begin to read without prior consideration. Rather, let the weekly reader begin on Sunday <with a blessing>. ²After Mass and Communion, let him seek the prayers of all, so that almighty God will remove from him the spirit of vanity. ³And let him begin this verse—*Lord, open my lips, and my mouth will proclaim your praise"*—*and let it be said three times by all.¹⁶⁶ ⁴Thus with a blessing let him begin his service as reader.

⁵Let there be a profound silence at meals, so that no one's voice or whispers may be heard except the reader's.¹⁶⁷ ⁷If they have need of anything as they eat or drink, let them ask for it with some sign and not with

*Ps 50 [51]:17

---

¹⁶⁵ "they . . . life": translating *RB 1980* 37.1, "tamen et regulae auctoritas eis prospiciat" ("the authority of the rule should also provide for them").

¹⁶⁶ Omitting *RB 1980* 38.3, "in oratorio" ("in the oratory").

¹⁶⁷ "at meals": translating the *receptus* and *interpolatus* reading "ad mensam," which *RB 1980* 38.5 omits.

the voice.[168] [8]And let no one presume to inquire about the reading or any other thing, *lest occasion be given.** [9]However, the superior may desire to explain the reading briefly for their spiritual instruction.[169]

*Eph 4:27; 1 Tim 5:14

[10]Let the weekly reader receive some bread and something to drink before he begins reading, because of his partaking in Holy Communion and so that he will not consider his fast too long. [11]After the reading he may eat with the attendants.

[12]Brothers will read and sing not according to their rank. Rather, those who are recognized as capable and as edifying to others will be chosen.

XXXIX. Concerning the Proper Amount of Food

[1]We believe that two kinds of cooked dishes at the daily meals are enough to accommodate individual weaknesses.[170] [2]If someone cannot enjoy one <on account of his fastidiousness>, he may enjoy the other. [3]If fruit or other fresh foods are available, they may

[168] Omitting *RB 1980* 38.6, "Quae vero necessaria sunt . . . sic sibi vicissim ministrent fratres ut nullus indigeat petere aliquid" ("The brothers should by turn serve one another's needs . . . so that no one need ask for anything") and placing *RB 1980* 38.6, "comedentibus et bibentibus" ("as they eat or drink"), into *RB 1980* 38.7.

[169] "However . . . instruction": translating *RB 1980* 38.9, "nisi forte prior pro aedificatione voluerit aliquid breviter dicere" ("The superior, however, may wish to say a few words of instruction"). Here Æthelwold makes the Lat "pro aedificatione" more explicit by modifying OE ȝetimbrung with the OE adjective ȝastlic ("spiritual") (cf. his note on biblical exegesis in "King Edgar's Establishment of Monasteries" in Appendix 3 below).

[170] Omitting *RB 1980* 39.1, "tam sextae quam nonae, omnibus mensis" ("whether at noon or in midafternoon . . . all tables").

have a third dish.[171] [4]Let there be a pound of bread for the whole day.[172] [5]If they eat two meals, let a third portion of the pound be reserved for supper.[173]

[6]If they are beset with difficult work—so that they require more than normal—the abbot judges what the additional sustenance will be, [7]provided that they do not overindulge, [8]for nothing is so hurtful and grievous to Christians as overindulgence. [9]Concerning this our Savior says, *Take care that your hearts are not oppressed by overindulgence.**

*Luke 21:34

[10]Young boys should not be given the same amount of food as their elders but less so that <both elders and juniors> ever hold to frugality. [11]Let everyone equally abstain from meat completely, except those who are weak and the sick.

XL. Concerning the Proper Amount of Drink

[1]*Everyone has his particular gift from God, and some are greater than others.*[174]* [2]Therefore I establish the proper amount of food and drink for others with some hesitation. [3]However, with due regard for the sick and the weak, we believe that the measure of wine known as a hemina is sufficient for each monk's daily drink,[175]

*1 Cor 7:7

---

[171] Omitting *RB 1980* 39.3, "Ergo duo pulmentaria cocta fratribus omnibus sufficiant" ("Two kinds of cooked food, therefore, should suffice for all the brothers").

[172] Omitting *RB 1980* 39.4, "sive una sit refectio sive prandii et cenae" ("whether for only one meal or for both dinner and supper").

[173] "If they eat two meals": replacing *RB 1980* 39.5, "quod si cenaturi sunt" ("if they will eat supper" [my translation]). Omitting *RB 1980* 39.5, "a cellarario" ("the cellarer").

[174] "*Everyone . . . others*": translating *RB 1980* 40.1, "*Unusquisque proprium habet donum ex Deo, alius sic, alius vero sic*" ("*Everyone has his own gift from God, one this and another that*").

[175] "hemina": While there is no certainty as to the amount Benedict intended in RB, Æthelwold does not attempt to trans-

⁴though those who patiently abstain from wine should know that God will give them their own great reward.¹⁷⁶

⁵It is up to the abbot's judgment whether local conditions, work, or the summer heat indicates a need for a greater amount. And he should take care lest, with this additional amount, overindulgence creep in and deceive them.¹⁷⁷ ⁶Though we read that wine is in no way a drink appropriate for monks, yet monks in our day cannot be persuaded of this. And so we grant permission to drink it in such a manner that being full is not taken to its own fullness!¹⁷⁸ One should always

---

late the Lat word into OE but rather borrows the word as OE *emina*. Since it is not clear from other Anglo-Saxon texts what *hemina* meant to Æthelwold, I have retained his direct borrowing. For knowledge of the term and its meaning, see the note to *RB 1980* 40.3 and the references included there. We can presume that Æthelwold would have received his understanding of *hemina* from Smaragdus, Expositio 40.4 (258; Comm 411), "'Emina' enim vini 'adpendit libram unam, quae geminate sextarium facit'" ("A 'hemina' of wine 'weighs one pound, and when doubled makes a *sextarius* [a pint]'"), which Smaragdus derives from Isidore of Seville's *Etymologiae*.

¹⁷⁶ "though. . . reward": translating *RB 1980* 40.4, "Quibus autem donat Deus tolerantiam abstinentiae, propriam se habituros mercedem sciant" ("But those to whom God gives the strength to abstain must know that they will earn their own reward").

¹⁷⁷ "overindulgence . . . them": translating *RB 1980* 40.5, "ne surrepat satietas aut ebrietas" ("lest excess or drunkenness creep in").

¹⁷⁸ "And . . . fullness": translating *RB 1980* 40.6, "saltem vel hoc consentiamus ut non usque ad satietatem bibamus, sed parcius" ("let us at least agree to drink moderately, and not to the point of excess"). Though this phrasing is perhaps a bit awkward, I have translated this passage rather literally in order to bring out the paronomasia Æthelwold employs. Here he translates Lat "satietatem" ("excess," or simply "the state of being sated") literally with the OE noun *fyl* ("being full"), with the OE reading "þæt þær næfre seo fyl be fullum ne weorðe." Making *fyl* the subject of the clause instead of the object, he

drink with restraint, taking less than one desires, [7]for
wine makes even the wise go astray <and turn from right
Sir 19:2   belief>.

[8]However, if a locale's poverty necessitates that the
monks cannot receive the full amount but rather much
less or even none, let those who live there bless their
Lord, not grumble <or complain in their minds>.[179]
[9]Above all things we admonish them not to grumble.

XLI. Concerning the Times for Meals

[1]From holy Easter until Pentecost, the brothers eat
two meals: one at noon and the other in the evening.
[2]From Pentecost throughout the summer they fast
<two days a week—that is>, on Wednesday and Fri-
day—unless they have excessive work or the summer
heat could harm them.[180]

[3]On the other days they eat two meals—that is, at
midday and again in the evening.[181] [4]If they have work
in the fields or if the summer heat remains oppressive,
the abbot may decide to continue the meal at midday.
[5]He should so regulate and arrange all things that

---

plays with the OE adjective *full* ("complete," or "fullest state of
something") by making this similar-sounding word the subject's
contrasting element. He clearly intended this pun to stand out,
since he translates Benedict's Latin very loosely in order to do
so, and the Latin text has no pun. Though this wordplay is not
perhaps to modern taste, we do see in this transformation of
RB a hint of humor or playfulness on Æthelwold's part.

[179] "or complain in their minds": Here Æthelwold may have
drawn on Smaragdus, Expositio 40.9 (259; Comm 413), in which
Smaragdus quotes Jude 16, "*murmuratores, querelosi*" ("*murmur-
ers, complainers*").

[180] Omitting *RB 1980* 41.2, "ad nonam" ("until midafternoon").

[181] "On . . . evening": translating *RB 1980* 41.3, "reliquis die-
bus ad sextam prandeant" ("On the other days they eat dinner
at noon").

souls may be saved and that the brothers may work without grumbling.[182]

⁶From the Ides of September until the beginning of Lent they eat one meal in midafternoon.[183] ⁷Throughout Lent until Easter, they fast until evening. ⁸Let Vespers be so performed that they have no need of candlelight at their meal.[184] Rather, let everything be finished by daylight. ⁹It should always be so arranged that, whether there be one or two meals, everything may be set in order by daylight.[185]

XLII. Concerning the Monks' Silence after Compline

¹Monks should cultivate silence at all times, but especially at night. ²⁻³Whether they fast or not, they shall arise immediately after their evening meal once they have eaten and sit together in one place. Someone should read from the *Conferences* or the *Lives of the Fathers*, or something that draws them to God.[186] ⁴They should not read the books of Moses or Kings, for those who lack understanding will have a difficult time detecting the spiritual sense [of these books] without the exposition of holy men.[187] Yet they should read

---

[182] Omitting *RB 1980* 41.5, "iusta" ("justified"), referring to "grumbling."

[183] Omitting *RB 1980* 41.6, "semper" ("always").

[184] "candlelight": translating *RB 1980* 41.8, "lumen lucernae" ("the light of an oil lamp" [my translation]).

[185] "whether . . . meals": translating *RB 1980* 41.9, "sive cena sive refectionis hora" ("supper or the hour of the fast-day meal").

[186] "draws them to God": translating *RB 1980* 42.3, "aedificet audientes" ("will benefit the hearers").

[187] "Books of Moses": translating *RB 1980* 42.4, "Heptateuchum" ("the Heptateuch").

these books at other times in church, when it is appropriate.[188]

⁵On fast days there should be a short interval between the singing of Vespers and when they go to hear
the readings as indicated above.[189] ⁷Let the whole
congregation gather for the reading. Whatever is entrusted to each one in obedience, let him lay it aside

---

[188] "Yet . . . appropriate": translating *RB 1980* 42.4, "non
autem Heptateuchum aut Regum, quia infirmis intellectibus
non erit utile illa hora hanc scripturam audire, aliis vero horis
legantur" ("but not the Heptateuch or the Books of Kings, because it will not be good for those of weak understanding to
hear these writings at that hour; they should be read at other
times"), by drawing on, but altering the sense of, Smaragdus,
Expositio 42.4–5 (262–63; Comm 419), "Cum vero dicit *Non
autem Eptaticum aut Regum*, diligenter adtendendum est quod
sequitur. *Quia infirmis* inquit *intellectibus non erit utile illa hora
hanc scripturam audire.* Sinceris autem, sanis et acutis intellectibus nullo tempore vetatur Eptaticum aut Regum vel
quamcumque historiam divinarum legere scripturarum, quia
possunt in eis figuras et sensus dinoscere et exemplum salutis
ab illis legendo recipere. Illis vero qui nequeunt ab illis spiri-
talem capere intellegentiam, Eptaticum aut Regum in illa hora
iuste prohibit legendum . . . . Ceterum aliis horis aut coram
omnibus tempore suo in ecclesia aut unusquisque pro legendi
doctrina debet eos legere in scola" ("But when he says, *But not
the Heptateuch or the Books of Kings,* we must pay careful attention
to what follows. He says, *Because it will not be helpful for weak
minds to hear this Scripture at that hour.* At no time are sincere,
sound, and sharp minds forbidden to read the Heptateuch or
Kings or any history whatever of the divine Scriptures, because
they are able to distinguish in them various figures and senses
and derive from them in their reading an example of salvation.
But he rightly forbids those who are not able to draw from them
a spiritual understanding to read the Heptateuch or Kings at
that hour . . . . For the rest, they are to be read at other hours,
either in the presence of everyone at their due time in the
church, or else each one must read them in school as part of
their learning to read").

[189] Omitting *RB 1980* 42.5, "Collationum" ("*Conferences*").

and come to the reading with haste.[190] [6]They should read four or five pages, or as many as daylight allows, from the prepared book.[191] [8]Together they should sing Compline <and the prayers of that canonical hour, possessing one mind* and being filled with compunction>. After Compline, no one will be allowed to speak a word [10]unless it happens that a guest arrives unexpectedly and the abbot commands something regarding the guest's needs. [11]This command should be carried out discreetly, with great modesty and gravity.[192] [9]If anyone breaks the silence prescribed by the rule, let him be subjected to severe punishment.[193]

*see Phil 2:2

---

[190] "Let . . . haste": translating *RB 1980* 42.7, "omnibus in unum occurrentibus per hanc moram lectionis, si qui forte in assignato sibi commisso fuit occupatus" ("This reading period will allow for all to come together, in case any were engaged in assigned tasks"), which here is placed before the translation of *RB 1980* 42.6 (see next note).

[191] "They . . . book": translating *RB 1980* 42.6, "Et lectis quattuor aut quinque foliis vel quantum hora permittit" ("Then let four or five pages be read, or as many as time permits"), which here is placed after the translation of *RB 1980* 42.7 (see previous note).

[192] "unless . . . gravity": translating *RB 1980* 42.10-11, "excepto si necessitas hospitum supervenerit aut forte abbas alicui aliquid iusserit, quod tamen et ipsud cum summa gravitate et moderatione honestissima fiat" ("except on occasions when guests require attention or the abbot wishes to give someone a command, but even this is to be done with the utmost seriousness and proper restraint"), which here is placed before the translation of *RB 1980* 42.9 (see next note).

[193] "If . . . punishment": translating *RB 1980* 42.9, "quod si inventus fuerit quisquam praevaricare hanc taciturnitatis regulam, gravi vindictae subiaceat" ("If anyone is found to transgress this rule of silence, he must be subjected to severe punishment"), which here is placed after the translation of *RB 1980* 42.11 (see previous note).

XLIII. Concerning Those Who Arrive Late to the Canonical Hours and the Prayer at Meals

[1]As soon as the ringing of the bell is heard, one must immediately lay down whatever he has in hand and go with haste to the canonical hour of the Divine Office.[194] [2]But let him hasten with gravity, not heedlessly. <He must not run, lest his heavy breathing cause nausea or heartburn.>[195] [3]Nothing is to be preferred to the Work of God, <nothing so loved that he would neglect his canonical hour>.

[4]One who comes late to the beginning of Vigils, before the *Gloria* of Psalm 94—which we wish to be sung slowly therefore—may not stand in choir in his normal place and order. [5]Rather, he must stand in the last place or the place the abbot has set aside for negligent people so that he may be shamed before the abbot and all his brothers [6]and at the end of the canonical hour openly make amends in penance—<that is, prostrate himself at the end of the canonical hour and humbly amend his negligence with visible penance>. [7]Therefore we have decided that they should stand in the last place or apart from the others, so that on account of their shame and fear of those who see them, they may amend their ways <and come more quickly to God's service>. [8]For if we should assign that they remain outside of the church, it is likely that some will lazily lie down and sleep, or else they might sit and speak idly, thus *giving occasion to the evil one* to do great

---

[194] "ringing of the bell": translating *RB 1980* 43.1, "signus" ("signal").

[195] The dependent clause in this sentence is obscure; my translation here is based on the best guess in Joseph Bosworth, *An Anglo-Saxon Dictionary: Based on the Manuscript Collections of the Late Joseph Bosworth*, ed. Thomas Northcote Toller (Oxford: Clarendon Press, 1898), s.v. *sogoþa*. Gretsch notes that this is probably a place where Æthelwold has misunderstood Benedict's Latin (Trans, 147).

damage.* ⁹Rather, he [*sic*] should go in so that he does
not completely lose the canonical hour and, though
he neglected the beginning, he may fulfill [the rest]
and amend in the future.¹⁹⁶

*Eph 4:27;
1 Tim 5:14

¹⁰At the daytime hours, [the monk] who arrives
after the beginning of the canonical hour—before the
Gloria of the first psalm is sung—should stand in the
last place, as we said above. ¹¹He should not presume
to join the choir or stand in his normal place, unless
the abbot grants him permission. ¹²Even if leave is
granted in this manner, [the monk] should follow the
aforesaid remedy and admit his guilt humbly.¹⁹⁷

¹³Anyone who is not present for the prayer at meals
¹⁴but through some vice or fault does not give thanks
to his Lord—who is the giver of all food—together
with his brothers should be verbally corrected twice.¹⁹⁸
¹⁵If he does not amend after this punishment, he
should not be permitted at the common table with his

---

¹⁹⁶ "For . . . damage": freely translating *RB 1980* 43.8-9, "nam,
si foris oratorium remaneant, erit forte talis qui se aut recollocet
et dormit, aut certe sedit sibi foris vel fabulis vacat, et *datur
occasio maligno*; sed ingrediantur intus, ut nec totum perdant et
de reliquo emendent" ("Should they remain outside the oratory,
there may be those who would return to bed and sleep, or,
worse yet, settle down outside and engage in idle talk, thereby
giving occasion to the Evil One. They should come inside so that
they will not lose everything and may amend in the future").

¹⁹⁷ "[the monk] . . . humbly": translating *RB 1980* 43.12, "ita
tamen ut satisfaciat reus ex hoc" ("Even in this case, the one at
fault is still bound to satisfaction").

¹⁹⁸ "Anyone . . . twice": translating *RB 1980* 43.13-14, "Ad
mensam autem qui ante versu non occurrerit, ut simul omnes
dicant versu et orent et sub uno omnes accedant ad mensam,
qui per neglegentiam suam aut vitio non occurrerit, usque se-
cunda vice pro hoc corripiatur" ("But, if anyone does not come
to the table before the verse so that all may say the verse and
pray and sit down at table together, and if this failure happens
through the individual's own negligence or fault, he should be
reproved up to the second time").

brothers [16]but should be kept apart. His portion of food and drink should be reduced until he makes amends for his careless fault.[199] [17]Anyone not present for the verse said after meals should undergo the same punishment and emendation.

[18]Let no one presume to partake of anything—food or drink—before or after the set time. [19]If anyone is offered something by an elder and he resentfully refuses it, he should not receive something else that he prefers at a meal or another time. Rather, he should receive what he was offered originally, once he makes appropriate amends in penance.[200]

---

[199] "His . . . fault": translating *RB 1980* 43.16, "sublata ei portione sua vinum, usque ad satisfactionem et emendationem" ("His portion of wine should be taken away until there is satisfaction and amendment").

[200] "If . . . amends": translating *RB 1980* 43.19, "sed et cui offertur aliquid a priore et accipere renuit, hora qua desideraverit hoc quod prius recusavit aut aliud, omnino nihil percipiat usque ad emendationem congruam" ("Moreover, if anyone is offered something by a superior and refuses it, then, if later he wants what he refused or anything else, he should receive nothing at all until he has made appropriate amends"). Here, especially in inserting the OE prepositional phrase *mid ȝebelȝe* ("resentfully"), it appears that Æthelwold attempts to clarify Benedict's point, drawing on Smaragdus and the latter's drawing on Basil. These refer to the need for the junior's "vice" to be "cured," suggesting that the need for amends is not simply because the junior refused but because he did so out of willfulness of one kind or another. See Smaragdus, Expositio 43.18 (267; Comm 426–27), "Hinc beatus Basilius ait, 'Hoc enim quod hic de esca dictum est, etiam de omni re quae ad usus corporis pertinent eadem forma servari potest.' Ergo, 'iste talis qui oblata recipere rennuit, dignus est ut etiamsi quaerat non accipiat usquequo probet is qui praeest; et cum viderit vitium animi curatum, tunc etiam quod corporis usibus necessarium fuerit praebebit'" ("And so blessed Basil says, 'What has here been said about food can also be kept in the same form concerning everything that pertains to the body's needs. Therefore [*sic*], such a one as refuses to accept what has been offered does not deserve to receive it even if he asks for it, until the one in charge

XLIV. Concerning How the Excommunicated Make Satisfaction

[1-2]Those who are excluded from the church or the common table because of grievous and serious faults should, at the end of each canonical hour, lie down at the church door and tremble, prostrate, at the brothers' feet as they leave the church, saying nothing. [3]They should continue to do so until the abbot decides that they have made satisfaction. [4]Next, [the guilty brother] should be offered the remedy of coming to the abbot's feet and then the feet of all the brothers, asking them all to intercede with God for him in prayer.[201] [5]After this, if the abbot deems it appropriate, he may take up a position in the choir that the abbot chooses. [6]Even so, he should not lead a service in the church on his own before the abbot bids it.[202] [7]But let him prostrate himself completely in his place at the end of each canonical hour and make satisfaction with penance in this manner [8]until the abbot decides he has made amends and orders him to stop.

[9]Those excommunicated from the common meals for lesser faults should make satisfaction in the church in a similar way, [10]doing so at the abbot's behest until he blesses them and says, "You have made amends."[203]

---

tests him; and if he sees that the mind's vice has been cured, then he will also give him what is required for the body's needs'").

[201] "asking . . . prayer": translating *RB 1980* 44.4, "ut orent pro ipso" ("that they may pray for him").

[202] "he . . . own": translating *RB 1980* 44.6, "ita sane ut psalmum aut lectionem vel aliud quid non praesumat in oratorio imponere" ("Even so, he should not presume to lead a psalm or a reading or anything else in the oratory").

[203] "You have made amends": translating *RB 1980* 44.10, "Sufficit" ("Enough").

XLV. Concerning Mistakes in the Church

¹If a brother errs and makes a mistake reciting a psalm, response, refrain, or reading and does not humble himself in penance before everyone there, he should receive a more severe and harsher punishment ²since he does not wish to remedy his fault with humility.[204] ³Young men should suffer blows for such faults.

XLVI. Concerning Faults in Minor Matters

¹The brother whose guilt is made known to the abbot and the brothers through another and not on his own must receive a greater and more severe punishment—²whether he neglects, forgets, or breaks anything in his charge, and whether he is occupied in the kitchen, the storeroom, the monastery's bakery, or the garden, or in any craft in which he is occupied in physical labor.[205] ⁴Let him receive a more severe punishment if he will not make known his own fault.

⁵If the faults of his soul are hidden from others yet known to himself, let him reveal it <in confession> to

---

[204] Omitting *RB 1980* 45.2, "quod negligentia deliquit" ("the wrong committed through negligence").

[205] "The brother . . . labor": translating *RB 1980* 46.1-3, "Si quis dum in labore quovis, in coquina, in cellario, in ministerio [see below], in pistrino, in horto, in arte aliqua dum laborat, vel in quocumque loco, aliquid deliquerit, aut fregerit quippiam aut perdiderit, vel aliud quid excesserit ubiubi, et non veniens continuo ante abbatem vel congregationem ipse ultro satisfecerit et prodiderit delictum suum" ("If someone commits a fault while at any work—while working in the kitchen, in the storeroom, in serving, in the bakery, in the garden, in any craft or anywhere else—either by breaking or losing something or failing in any other way in any other place, he must at once come before the abbot and community and of his own accord admit his fault and make satisfaction"). "monastery's bakery": translating the *receptus* and *interpolatus* reading "in monasterio in pistrino" ("in the monastery's bakery") instead of *RB 1980* 46.1, "in ministerio, in pistrino" ("in serving, in the bakery").

his abbot or a spiritual brother ⁶who is <salutary>, knowing how to heal his <soul's> wounds and to keep such things to himself.[206]

XLVII. Concerning the Announcement of the Hours for the Work of God

¹It is in the abbot's care that [the bell] for all the hours of the divine service be rung at the correct and proper time, whether he signals each hour himself or entrusts this charge to a very conscientious brother.[207] He will make every hour known at the appropriate time and will not neglect any hour of the divine service.[208]

²[Brothers] who are bidden will begin the psalms and refrains in their order after the abbot. ³No one should presume either to read or sing unless he can fulfill that service in such a way that he <will not vex but rather> may edify those who listen.[209]

XLVIII. Concerning the Daily Work and When They Are to Read

¹Idleness is the enemy of the soul. Therefore the brothers should have allotted times for manual labor and *lectio divina*.[210]

---

[206] Omitting *RB 1980* 46.6, "detegere" ("exposing").

[207] "[the bell] . . . rung": translating *RB 1980* 47.1, "Nuntianda" ("to announce")

[208] "He . . . service": translating *RB 1980* 47.1, "ut omnia horis competentibus compleantur" ("so that everything may be done at the proper time").

[209] Omitting *RB 1980* 47.4, "quod cum humilitate et gravitate et tremore fiat, et cui iusserit abbas" ("let this be done with humility, seriousness, and reverence, and at the abbot's bidding").

[210] "*lectio divina*": translating OF *godcundre rædinʒe*, itself a literal translation of *RB 1980* 48.1, "lectione divina"; rather than

²We believe that the times for both these kinds <of work> may be arranged thus: ³from Easter until the calends of October, as soon as they leave Prime they are to work on whatever needs to be done until the fourth hour. ⁴Then they read their books until midday. ⁵After midday, once they have eaten, they can go to their beds in complete silence. If someone wants to read on his bed, let him do so in a manner that does not disturb others with noise. ⁶None is announced and said early, about half past the eighth hour, after which they work at whatever is needed until the evening. ⁷If local conditions necessitate that they must do the harvesting themselves and they are occupied with this, they must not be distressed. ⁸For they are true monks if they live by the work of their hands, just as our fathers and the apostles did. ⁹Yet all things should be done in moderation, lest the fainthearted despair.[211]

¹⁰From the calends of October until the Lenten fast, they read their books until the hour before Terce.[212] ¹¹After [Terce] they work at their assigned tasks until None. ¹²Once they hear the first sound of the bell, everyone leaves his work and prepares to go to the church at the second ringing.[213] ¹³After their repast at None, they read their books again or sing their psalms.

¹⁴During the Lenten fast they should read their books from dawn almost until None and then work at whatever is needed until an hour after None. ¹⁵During

---

guess at precisely what nuance Æthelwold had in mind regarding this practice, I employ the contemporary English strategy of retaining the Latin.

[211] "lest the fainthearted despair": translating *RB 1980* 48.9, "propter pusillanimes" ("on account of the fainthearted").

[212] "Lenten fast": translating *RB 1980* 48.10, "quadragesimae" ("Lent") as OE *lenctenfæst* ("Lenten fast"), though OE *lencten* ("Lent") would work just as well.

[213] "sound of the bell" and "ringing": translating *RB 1980* 48.12, "signo" and "signum" ("signal") as OE *cnyll* (literally "knell").

the days of the fast, each should take a book from the library and read it.[214] [16]These are distributed at the beginning of Lent.

[17]While the brothers are reading, let there be one or two wise elders who go throughout the monastery [18]and make sure that no brother is engaged in idle or useless talk instead of his reading, thus making himself useless not only to himself but also to others. [19]If someone is found conducting himself in this manner —God forbid—let him be rebuked once and twice.[215] [20]If he will not amend, he must be subjected to the discipline of the rule so that the others may have a greater fear.[216] [21]Brothers should not associate with one another or have fellowship at inappropriate times.

[22]On Sundays the brothers read holy books, except those who have been entrusted with other tasks.[217] [23]If any brother is found to be so negligent and idle that he will not or cannot study or read holy books, he should be given other work that he might not be idle.

[24]Sick or weak brothers should be given some simple and light work to keep them occupied, lest the immoderation or harshness of the work overwhelm them and they seek to flee their burden. [25]The abbot must always consider their infirmities.

[214] "and read it": translating *RB 1980* 48.15, "quos per ordinem ex integro legant" ("and is to read the whole of it straight through").

[215] "God forbid": translating *RB 1980* 48.19, "quod absit" ("the which be absent" [my translation]) literally, but I translate the OE with the customary Modern English translation of "quod absit," i.e., "God forbid," used also in *RB 1980*.

[216] "a greater fear": translating *RB 1980* 48.20, "timeant" ("that they may fear" [my translation]) with a comparative.

[217] "the brothers read holy books": translating *RB 1980* 48.22, "lectioni vacent omnes" ("all are to be engaged in reading").

XLIX. Concerning the Observance of Lent

[1]Monks should practice the restraint of fasting at all times—[2]and too few observe such a strenuous life.[218] Still, they should most vigorously practice the cleansing of restraint during the Lenten fast, [3]so that they may blot out in these holy days what they neglected at other times in their carelessness. [4]This is done in a fitting manner if they restrain themselves from every sin and vice, if they [devote themselves] eagerly to spiritual reading, holy prayers, and compunction of heart.[219] [5]During these days they will add something to their usual service: they will practice restraint in food and drink [6]so that each will, of his own will, have something beyond the assigned measure of his sustenance to offer God *with the joy of the Holy Spirit.*[220]* [7]They should eagerly observe additional private prayer and practice restraint in food, drink, or sleep. They should also eagerly guard against <the frivolity of> idle words and unprofitable conduct <at this and at all times>, that they may look forward to Easter with the joy of spiritual longing.[221]

[8]And so that they may consider well what they will give up, they should seek the abbot's permission and consent. [9]Whatever is done without his permission

*1 Thess 1:6

---

[218] "Monks . . . life": translating *RB 1980* 49.1-2, "Licet omni tempore vita monachi quadragesimae debet observationem habere, tamen, quia paucorum est ista virtus" ("The life of a monk should be a continuous Lent. Since few, however, have the strength for this").

[219] "if . . . heart": translating *RB 1980* 49.4, "orationi cum fletibus, lectioni et compunctioni cordis atque abstinentiae" ("by devoting ourselves to prayer with tears, to reading, to compunction of heart and self-denial").

[220] Omitting *RB 1980* 49.5, "orationes peculiares" ("private prayer"), but this is moved to the head of the list in the translation of *RB 1980* 49.7.

[221] "that they": translating the *receptus* and *purus* reading "ut" ("that") instead of *RB 1980* 49.7, "et" ("and").

and consent is to be reckoned as negligent and idle vainglory rather than as an offering.[222] [10]Everything that they do must be done with the abbot's permission.

L. Concerning Brothers Working at a Distance from the Church

[1]Brothers who work so far away that they cannot get back to the church for the appointed canonical hours on account of the distance—[2]if the abbot decides that this is the case—[3]perform the hours where they are at work and humbly kneel in fear of God.[223]

[4]Those on a journey should do likewise, not neglecting the prescribed hours but performing each one as best they can. They should not neglect the usual course of their service on account of their work nor on account of a journey.[224]

LI. Concerning Brothers Sent on a Journey

[1]Brothers who go out on some errand and can return to the monastery the same day should not presume to eat outside of the monastery, even if someone asks, [2]unless ordered to do so by their abbot.[225] [3]If someone

[222] "an offering": translating *RB 1980* 49.9, "mercedi" ("reward"), as OE *ælmessan*, which is generally translated "almsgiving" but here seems to imply "something that is offered in a worthy manner."

[223] "the hours": translating *RB 1980* 50.3, "opus Dei" ("Work of God").

[224] "They . . . journey": translating *RB 1980* 50.4, "et servitutis pensum non neglegant reddere" ("not neglecting their measure of service").

[225] "go out": translating the *receptus* reading "profiscuntur" ("go out") instead of *RB 1980* 51.1, "diiigltur" ("is sent").

presumes to do this without his permission, he should be excommunicated.

LII. Concerning the Monastery's Oratory

¹The oratory should be only what it is called, and nothing else should be done or stored there <except the work belonging to God—that is, prayer>. ²At the end of each canonical hour, everyone should leave in complete silence with reverence for God ³so that a brother who desires to pray to God privately will not be hindered or prevented by the impropriety of another. ⁴If at another time someone desires to be alone to pray secretly, he may simply go in silently and pray, not with a loud voice but with tears and custody of his heart <and all his thoughts>. ⁵Therefore, anyone who will not take up this work in this manner should leave once the canonical hour has ended, lest he hinder those devoted to private prayer.[226]

LIII. Concerning the Reception of Guests

*Matt 25:35

¹All guests who come to the monastery should be received as Christ himself, for he says in the holy gospel, *I was a stranger, and you received me.*[227]* ²The same fitting honor must be shown *to all, but especially to those*

[226] "lest . . . prayer": translating *RB 1980* 52.5, "ne alius impedimentum paitatur" ("then he will not interfere with anyone else"); omitting *RB 1980* 52.5, "sicut dictum est" ("as we have said").

[227] The word translated here as "stranger," OE *cuma*, is the same as the word translated "guest," just as is the case in *RB 1980*, which uses Lat *hospes* for both. For consistency with current usage, I have translated these two uses differently, as does *RB 1980*.

who share the true faith and those who are exiled or are abroad as pilgrims.[228]* *Gal 6:10

³Therefore, as soon as a guest has been announced, the superior or the brothers go to him with all the service of charity. ⁴First they pray together and so assemble in true peace. ⁵But they should not offer the kiss of peace before they have prayed to God and received a blessing, because of the devil's various deceits.

⁶All humility is to be shown to every guest who comes to the monastery or leaves it. ⁷<Humbly> bowing the head or prostrating the entire body upon the floor, they worship Christ, who is always received in guests, <with humility>. ⁸Let them be led to the church for prayer, and once they have been received let the superior or an appointed brother sit with them. ⁹The divine law and teaching are read to the guest so that he may be encouraged toward God's will, after which let all kindness be shown to him as is appropriate. ¹⁰The superior may break his fast for the sake of the guest, unless it is a special fast day that cannot be broken. ¹¹The brothers, however, observe the usual fast. ¹²The abbot should pour water on the guests' hands, ¹³and either the abbot or the whole community washes the guests' feet. ¹⁴After this washing they say this verse: *We have received your mercy, Lord, in the midst of your temple.** *Ps 47 [48]:10

¹⁵The abbot must have the greatest care for the reception of the poor and pilgrims, for Christ is received more particularly in them. Our fear of the rich assures

---

²²⁸ "who are . . . pilgrims": my translation reflects the ambiguity of Æthelwold's Old English translation as well as the uncertainty of the Latin in *RB 1980*. Æthelwold's translation of *RB 1980* 53.2, "peregrinis" ("pilgrims")—*þam forwrecenum elþeodegum*—seems literally to mean something like "those who, being exiled, are far from their homeland." But for the problems of the term *peregrinus* in RB, see Fry, n. to 53 2.

that they will be worthily regarded <and shown honor enough, but the fear of God alone assures that we will be helpful to the poor and pilgrims>.

[16]The kitchen for the abbot and guests ought to be separate, so that the brothers are not disturbed when guests arrive suddenly at the monastery at unexpected times—monasteries are seldom without guests. [17]Each year, two brothers who know the tasks and can carry out the service well should be assigned to this kitchen. [18]Let them have help if it is needed, so that <with the ease this help provides> they may serve without grumbling. Once there is less work, let them go to whatever work they are ordered to out of obedience. [19]This consideration is not for them alone, but for all the monastery's servers. [20]When necessary they should receive help and support; when they are not busy with other duties and are unoccupied, they should do whatever they are ordered out of obedience.

[21]The guesthouse should be entrusted to the charge of a brother who is God-fearing <and has possession of his soul>. [22]There should always be a sufficient number of beds made there. The house of God, <which is the guesthouse>, should be wisely overseen by wise brothers.

[23]No one should associate with guests or speak with them unless it has been ordered. [24]If they meet a guest, they should greet him humbly, as we have said before. They should ask for a blessing and continue on, explaining that they are not allowed to speak with a guest.

LIV. Concerning How No Monk Should Receive Letters or Other Gifts

[1]No monk is ever allowed to send either a letter or [receive] a gift from his family or another person, nor to exchange such things, nor to give them, except at

the abbot's behest.[229] [2]If his family sends something he is not to presume to accept it before telling the abbot. [3]If the abbot orders him to accept it, it is his decision to whom the gift will be given. [4]And the brother to whom the gift was sent must not be distressed, *lest occasion be given to the devil* and he rejoice in that distress.* [5]The one who presumes to do differently must undergo the discipline of the rule.

*Eph 4:27;
1 Tim 5:14

LV. Concerning the Monks' Wardrobe and Clothing

[1]The clothing given to the brothers should vary according to the nature of the place in which they live, its region, and its weather. [2]In cold regions more clothing will be needed, in warm regions less. [3]The abbot must consider [the brothers'] needs. [4]Yet we believe that in temperate regions a cowl and a tunic will suffice for each monk. [5]In winter a thick cowl is needed, in summer a thin or an old worn one. [6]They must also have a scapular for work—<which is like a small cowl without sleeves>—and hose as well as shoes for footwear.[230]

[7]Monks must not complain about the color or coarseness of the clothing; they must use the kind of clothing found in the area in which they live and that can be purchased most cheaply. [8]The abbot should be

---

[229] "No . . . behest": translating *RB 1980* 54.1, "Nullatenus liceat monacho neque a parentibus suis neque a quoquam hominum nec sibi invicem litteras, eulogias vel quaelibet munuscula accipere aut dare sine praecepto abbatis" ("In no circumstances is a monk allowed, unless the abbot says he may, to exchange letters, blessed tokens, or small gifts of any kind, with his parents or anyone else, or with a fellow monk").

[230] "hose . . . footwear": translating *RB 1980* 55.6, "indumenta pedum pedules et caligas" ("and footwear—both sandals and shoes").

concerned about and regulate the measurement of the clothing, assuring that it is not too short but rather fitted to those who will wear it.

⁹When new clothing is received, the old items should always be returned and kept in the wardrobe to be distributed to the poor. ¹⁰For each monk, two cowls and two tunics are enough and, indeed, quite sufficient for nightwear and for laundering. ¹¹Everything in excess of this is to be considered idle and superfluous. If there is more it should be taken away. ¹²As often as they receive new shoes or any other new item, the old items must be returned.

¹³Those who go on a journey should receive underclothing from the wardrobe, and when they return home from their journey they should wash it. ¹⁴They should also receive from the wardrobe cowls and tunics that are somewhat better than those they normally wear. Those who go on journeys should receive these and return them back to the wardrobe when they have returned home.

¹⁵For bedding they will need a mat, blanket, a bed covering, and a pillow.

¹⁶Yet the abbot should frequently inspect the beds and search for private possessions. ¹⁷If someone has something or something is found in his bed that he has not received from his abbot, he must undergo the most serious and severe punishment. ¹⁸In order that this vice of private ownership may be reduced and blotted out, they are given everything they need by the abbot—¹⁹that is, cowl, tunic, shoes, hose, sleeves, belt, knife, stylus, needle, a handkerchief, wax tablets —so that every excuse for needing something may be blotted out <and they have no reason for private possessions>.²³¹

²³¹ "cowl . . . tablets": translating *RB 1980* 55.19, "cuculla, tunica, pedules, caligas, bracile, cultellum, graphium, acum, mappula, tabulas" ("cowl, tunic, sandals, shoes, belt, knife, stylus, needle, handkerchief, and writing tablets").

²⁰The abbot must always bear in mind and consider the saying that is written in the book called *Actus Apostolorum*, that is, *Distribution was made to each one as he required and had need.** ²¹In this way the abbot will also consider the infirmities of those who require attention because of need and poverty, not turning aside from their needs on account of the evil will of the envious. ²²In all his judgments let the abbot recall God's retribution—<that is, that he will be repaid at God's Judgment according to his former works>.

*Acts 4:35

LVI. Concerning the Abbot's Table

¹The abbot's table should always be filled with the needy and pilgrims.²³² ²When there are not many guests, let him invite some of the brothers. It lies in his judgment who these will be. ³However, one or two elders should remain with the brothers to watch over their conduct.

LVII. Concerning the Monastery's Craftsmen

¹If there are craftsmen in the monastery, they should practice their crafts and work at them eagerly, if it pleases the abbot. ²If someone exalts himself proudly on account of his craft and <because of this confidence> thinks that he is conferring something special on the place, ³he should no longer be permitted to practice his craft. He should not take up his craft again unless with great humility he obtains the abbot's permission.

⁴If anyone should sell something that the monastery's craftsmen have made, let those who make the sale take heed that they do nothing deceitful. ⁵They

²³² "the needy": translating *RB 1980* 56.1, "hospitibus" ("guests").

*Acts 5:1-11

should remember Ananias and Sapphira, who suffered bodily death,* ⁶lest they and anyone else who practices deceit in monastery affairs should suffer spiritual death.

⁷If anyone should need to sell something he has made, it should be sold without avarice ⁸and so at a lower price than those in the world [can set], ⁹*so that*
*1 Pet 4:11
*God's praise may abide in all things.*²³³*

LVIII. Concerning the Reception of New Brothers

¹If someone new desires to take up the monastic life, do not grant him an easy entrance. ²Rather, do as the apostle teaches—that is, eagerly *test them to see if they*
*1 John 4:1
*are filled with the Spirit of God.** ³If he patiently bears both reproach and scorn, enduring this difficulty and humbly persisting in his request that he be granted entry, let him be received only after four or five days.²³⁴ ⁴Then let him stay in the guesthouse for a few days. ⁵Then he should be taken to the novitiate, where he will eat, sleep, and consider his spiritual duty.²³⁵

⁶And an elder who is spiritually wise and knows well how to win souls for God will watch over him. ⁷He must eagerly attend to the one entrusted to his care and diligently observe whether or not he seeks God with sincere compunction and reverence, if he

---

²³³ "*so that . . . things*": translating *RB 1980* 57.9, "*ut in omnibus glorificetur Deus*" ("*so that in all things God may be glorified*").

²³⁴ "If . . . days": omitting *RB 1980* 58.3, "si veniens perseveraverit pulsans" ("if someone comes and keeps knocking at the door"), drawn from Luke 11:8.

²³⁵ "consider his spiritual duty": translating *RB 1980* 58.5, "meditent" ("study"). While *þearf*, the OE word translated here as "duty," generally means "need, something needful," it can also mean "what is required of someone, duty," the latter of which seems to me to be closer to the novice's task.

shows concern for and is quick to the Work of God and to obedience, and if he patiently endures reproach and scorn.[236] [8]He should be clearly told about the hardship and the difficulties that will lead him to God <and to the joy of the heavenly kingdom>.

[9]If he promises to be steadfast in his stability, after two months read this rule in his presence, [10]and say to him, "Here is the law; under its teaching you are choosing to strive and fight. If you can keep it, come in; if you cannot keep it, you are free to go where you will."[237] [11]If he still perseveres, let him be taken back to the novitiate and rigorously tested whether or not

[236] "And . . . scorn": freely translating and expanding upon *RB 1980* 58.6-7, "Et senior eis talis deputetur qui aptus sit ad lucrandas animas, qui super eos omnino curiose intendat. Et sollicitudo sit si revera Deum quaerit, si sollicitus est ad opus Dei, ad oboedientiam, ad opprobria" ("A senior chosen for his skill in winning souls should be appointed to look after them with careful attention. The concern must be whether the novice truly seeks God and whether he shows eagerness for the Work of God, for obedience and for trials").

[237] "Here . . . will": loosely translating and expanding upon *RB 1980* 58.10, "et dicatur ei: Ecce lex sub qua militare vis; si potes observare, ingredere; si vero non potes, liber discede" ("This is the law under which you are choosing to serve. If you can keep it, come in. If not, feel free to leave"). Note that Æthelwold this time emphasizes the martial aspect of Lat *militare* (which he plays down in his translation of *RB 1980* Prol. 3 and 2.20) by translating this Lat verb with two OE verbs, *winnan* ("strive") and *campiam* ("fight"), which together produce an unambiguously martial tone. In this, he is in sync with Smaragdus, Expositio 58.10 (293; Comm 470), "Notandum, quia non ait: Ecce lex sub qua quiescas vel vacans otio quietus vivas, sed *sub qua militare vis* inquit, ut intellegas quia 'militia est vita hominis super terram et sicut dies mercenarii dies eius'" ("It must be noted that he does not say: This is the law under which you may rest and live quietly and at leisure, but he says **under which you wish to do military service**, so that you may understand that *the life of man on earth is a military service, and his days are like the days of a mercenary*" [bold typeface reflects Barry's formatting]).

he is long-suffering and patient.[238] [12]Again after six months read this entire rule to him from the beginning so that he may more readily understand what he will be striving toward. [13]If he still perseveres, after four months let this rule be read to him again, and explain the meaning to him. [14]If then by his own choice he promises to observe everything and to fulfill all the rule's commands, let him be received into the community. [15]He must know that, as the bonds of the rule bind and establish, from that day forward he will not be able to leave the monastery [16]or shake or cast off from his neck this rule's yoke, since earlier he had the choice to accept or refuse it during a protracted period of consideration.

[17]When he is received and brought into the church, he promises to God and all his saints, before the entire community, that he will dwell in stability in the monastery, incline his conduct completely to God's will, and persevere in obedience.[239] [18]If at any point he breaks this promise, let him know that the almighty Lord, whom he mocks, will cast him down and humble him.[240] [19]He establishes this promise in a document in the name of the abbot and the saints whose relics—<that is, their bones>—rest in that place. [20]He writes this document with his own hand. If he does not know how to write, he asks someone who does to do it for him and then puts his sign on the document.[241] After this, he places it upon the altar with his own hands. [21]As soon as he places that document upon the altar, he begins this verse, saying, *Suscipe me,*

---

[238] "long-suffering and patient": translating *RB 1980* 58.11, "omni patientia" ("all patience").

[239] "incline . . . will": translating *RB 1980* 58.17, "conversatione morum suorum" ("fidelity to the monastic life").

[240] "the almighty Lord": freely translating the *interpolatus* and *receptus* reading "a Deo" ("by God") instead of *RB 1980* 58.18, "ab eo" ("by the one").

[241] "puts . . . document": omitting *RB 1980* 58.20, "novicius" ("the novice").

Domine, secundum eloquium tuum, et uiuam, et non con-
fundas me ab expectatione mea*—<which is, in our language, *Lord, receive me according to your promise, and I*
will live, and do not confound me in my hope>. ²²<He says
this verse three times, and> the entire community responds with the same verse three times and then adds,
Gloria Patri. ²³Once the new brother has been blessed,
he falls at the feet of each brother and asks for his
prayers. From that day on the brother is counted as
one of the community.

*Ps 118 [119]:116

²⁴If he has any property, he should either give it to
the poor beforehand or worthily entrust it to the monastery, retaining nothing for himself. ²⁵Indeed, from
that day forward he, in addition to possessing nothing
else, does not even have ownership of his own body.
²⁶At that time he should be stripped of the clothing
<he previously enjoyed> and be clothed in the mon-
astery's clothing.²⁴² ²⁷The clothing taken from him
should be held in the wardrobe ²⁸since, if he is ever
seduced by the devil's temptation <to consent to re-
nouncing his promise to God> and leaving the monastery—which God forbid—he should be deprived of
his godly clothing <and clothed again in his worldly
clothing that he formerly forsook>. In this way he
should be driven out of the monastery. ²⁹Even so, his
document should be kept at the monastery.²⁴³

LIX. Concerning the Offering of the Wealthy and the Poor

¹If a wealthy member of the nobility desires to offer
his son to God in the monastery and the child does
not possess the understanding to do so himself, his

²⁴² "At . . . monastery's clothing": omitting RB 58.26 "in oratorio" ("in the oratory").

²⁴³ Omitting *RB 1980* 58.29, "quam desuper altare abbas tulit,
non recipiat, sed" ("which the abbot took from the altar should
not be given back to him but").

parents establish his commitment at the presentation of the gifts. [2]That is, they wrap the child's hand and the document in the altar cloth and thus offer him to God along with the offering of the bread and wine.[244]

[3]The parents promise and establish with oaths that they will not give their son personal property either on their own or by means of an intermediary, nor will they seek an opportunity to enrich him by means of personal property. [4]If they desire to give him something, [5]they give it to the holy place as a possession in common, and this will be an eternal reward for them. Then they should be given food for their journey. If they want the food, they return home with it.[245] [6]All

---

[244] "If . . . wine": loosely translating *RB 1980* 59.1-2, "Si quis forte de nobilibus offerit filium suum Deo in monasterio, si ipse puer minor aetate est, parentes eius faciant petitionem quam supra diximus et cum oblatione ipsam petitionem et manum pueri involvant in palla altaris, et sic eum offerant" ("If a member of the nobility offers his son to God in the monastery, and the boy himself is too young, the parents draw up the document mentioned above; then, at the presentation of the gifts, they wrap the document itself and the boy's hand in the altar cloth. That is how they offer him"). "the offering of the bread and wine": making explicit the presumed meaning of *RB 1980* 59.2, "cum oblatione" ("at the presentation of the gifts," literally "with the oblation").

[245] "If they desire . . . with it": freely translating *RB 1980* 59.4-5, "vel certe si hoc facere noluerint et aliquid offerre volunt in eleemosynam monasterio pro mercede sua, faciant ex rebus quas dare volunt monasterio donationem, reservato sibi, si ita voluerint, usufructu" ("or else, if they are unwilling to do this and still wish to win their reward for making an offering to the monastery, they make a formal donation of the property that they want to give to the monastery, keeping the revenue for themselves, should they so desire"). Gretsch notes in *Trans* that this is probably a place where Æthelwold has misunderstood Benedict's Latin (147), yet later, in *Reform*, she reconsiders this alteration of RB as a sign of Æthelwold's acute concern to prevent the alienation of monastic property (131–38). I prefer the latter reading.

the property belonging to the child should be blotted out and divided in this manner so that he has no hope for personal property and so become lost. God forbid this, but we have frequently found <that many are lost through the hope of personal property>.

⁷Those who are poor and without property do similarly for their sons. If they have no property to give, they simply offer their sons in the presence of <catholic> witnesses.²⁴⁶

LX. Concerning Abbots and Other Distinguished People Who Desire to Live in the Monastery²⁴⁷

¹If a priest desires to receive the monastic state of life in the monastery, do not grant this too quickly just because he is a priest. ²If he persists in this desire, he [must know that] in his trial he may not neglect anything that the rule teaches. ³Rather, he must eagerly submit to each of the rule's customs and teachings. In keeping with the teaching of the gospel, he should be asked, *Friend, what have you come for?** <The sense of this is, "Do you come bringing peace and true compunction, or discord and duplicity?"> ⁴He should however be permitted to stand next to the abbot and sing Mass if the abbot so directs.²⁴⁸ ⁵He must always be willing to submit to the discipline of the rule's

*Matt 26:50

---

²⁴⁶ Omitting *RB 1980* 59.8, "petitionem faciant et cum oblatione" ("write the document and . . . with the gifts"). "catholic": I translate Æthelwold's OE *rihtȝelyfedum* as "catholic" rather than "orthodox" (which is closer to the literal sense), since he uses the same word to translate "catholicorum" ("catholic") on its own in *RB 1980* 73.4.

²⁴⁷ "abbots": this appears to be an error for "priests," but the manuscripts attest to this reading.

²⁴⁸ Omitting *RB 1980* 60.4, "et benedicere" ("to give blessings"). "sing Mass": translating RB 60.4, "missas tenere" ("celebrate Mass").

teaching and be so much the more humble as he is advanced in rank, ever offering himself as an example of humility to all those with whom he lives.[249] [6]If he has been granted a higher place because of the dignity of his state of life, [7]he should not dare—on account of this confidence invested in his state of life—to proceed further in the community's order than that determined by his conversion to monastic life. Rather, he should ever consider the place he holds according to his conversion to monastic life and be honored accordingly, except when he is granted a higher place on account of his priesthood.[250]

---

[249] "He . . . lives": freely translating *RB 1980* 60.5, "sin alias, ullatenus aliqua praesumat, sciens se disciplinae regulari subditum, et magis humilitatis exempla omnibus det" ("Otherwise, he must recognize that he is subject to the discipline of the rule, and not make any exceptions for himself, but rather give everyone an example of humility").

[250] "If . . . priesthood": expanding upon *RB 1980* 60.6-7, "Et si forte ordinationis aut alicuius rei causa fuerit in monasterio, illum locum attendat quando ingressus est in monasterio, non illum qui ei pro reverentia sacerdotii concessus est" ("Whenever there is a question of an appointment or of any other business in the monastery, he takes the place that corresponds to the date of his entry into the community, and not that granted him out of respect for his priesthood"). It appears that Æthelwold wants to make this statement clearer, and yet the repetitive quality of his expansion tends to obscure the basic point. However, it also seems that he understands this matter as Smaragdus does rather than the way Fry translates and explains it in *RB 1980*. In Smaragdus, Expositio 60.6 (304; Comm 487), as David Barry explains in his note to this verse, "Smaragdus clearly takes *causa* as an ablative modifying *ordinationis aut alicuius rei*, leaving an understood *sacerdos* as the subject of *fuerit*": "Quod dicit *si forte ordinationis*, aut quia sacerdos est ordinatus, aut quia ordinationis ministerium id est ut aliquid ordinaret potestatem accepti ab abbate in monasterio, *aut alicuius rei causa* subauditur fuerit exaltatus in monasterio, *illum locum adtendat*, et cetera" ("When he says *If perchance . . . [because] of ordination*, understand: either because he has been ordained priest, or because he has received a ministry of organizing, that is, he has received from the abbot authority to organize something in the monastery, *or [because*

[8]Clerics who desire to become monks should receive a place in the middle, as long as they promise to observe stability and the entirety of the holy rule.

LXI. Concerning How Visiting Monks Should Be Received

[1]If a monk visiting from unknown parts desires to stay as a guest [2]and does not disturb the monastery with excessive demands—[3]but rather is satisfied and content with the place's customs—he should be received and dwell there as long as he likes. [4]If he reasonably censures something or notes some problems in the monastery with humility and charity, the abbot should receive this with humility and consider that God may have sent him there to enrich and correct the place.[251]

[5]If at a later time he wants to bind himself to the monastery, his wish should not be refused, since there was time to assess his way of life while he dwelt in the monastery as a guest. [6]If during his time as a guest he has been found to be full of vices, he should not be permitted to associate himself with the monastery or the community.[252] [7]Rather, he should be told politely that he must depart, lest he corrupt others with his wretched ways.

---

of] something else, understand: he is placed high in rank in the monastery, *let him keep to that place,* and so forth"). In order to clarify the point I think Æthelwold is trying to make here, I translate his final conjunction, OE *butan* ("unless," "except"), as "except when."

[251] "the abbot . . . place": translating *RB 1980* 61.4, "tractet abbas prudenter ne forte pro hoc ipsud eum Dominus direxerit" ("which the abbot should prudently consider; it is possible that the Lord guided him to the monastery for this very purpose").

[252] Omitting *RB 1980* 61.6, "superfluus" ("excessive in his demands").

⁸If during his visit he proves that he is not someone worthy of being dismissed and yet does not ask to stay, he should be persuaded to remain there.²⁵³ ⁹In this way others may be taught and improved by his good example, ¹⁰because in every place we serve and obey one Lord and heavenly King.²⁵⁴ ¹¹If the abbot perceives that this man has the proper merit, he may honor him more and grant him a higher station and seat. ¹²This is not to be done only for monks, <but also for worthy canons who come into monastic life>.²⁵⁵ On account of their beneficial merit they are honored more—whether they be in priestly or clerical orders—if the abbot sees that his way of life merits it.²⁵⁶

²⁵³ "If . . . there": compressing *RB 1980* 61.8, "Quod si non fuerit talis qui mereatur proici, non solum si petierit suscipiatur congregationi sociandus, verum etiam suadeatur ut stet" ("If, however, he has shown that he is not the kind of man who deserves to be dismissed, let him, on his request, be received as a member of the community. He should even be urged to stay").

²⁵⁴ "we . . . King": translating *RB 1980* 61.10, "uni Domino servitor, uni regi militatur" ("we are in the service of the same Lord and doing battle for the same King").

²⁵⁵ "but . . . life": Here Æthelwold splices a comment about canons between *RB 1980* 61.12, "Non solum autem monachum" ("And not only for monks" [my translation]), and "sed etiam de suprascriptis gradibus sacerdotum vel clericorum" ("or someone in the priestly or clerical orders mentioned above"). That Æthelwold refers here to canons probably reflects the fact that during the Benedictine reform, many houses of canons were reformed as monasteries, Æthelwold himself, for instance, having dismissed the canons from the Old Minster in Winchester and replaced them with monks. For this movement more generally, see the introduction, section II.

²⁵⁶ "On . . . it": freely translating *RB 1980* 61.12, "sed etiam de suprascriptis gradibus sacerdotum vel clericorum stabilire potest abbas in maiori quam ingrediuntur loco, si eorum talem perspexerit esse vitam" ("or someone in the priestly or clerical orders mentioned above, the abbot has the power to set any of them above the place that corresponds to the date of his entry, if he sees that his life warrants it"). "his": translating the *receptus*

¹³The abbot must take heed, however, that he not receive any monk from a known monastery, unless the monk's abbot has given his permission and sent a letter, ¹⁴for it is written: *Do not do to others what you would not want done to yourself.**

*Tob 4:16

LXII. Concerning the Priests of the Monastery and Their Servants

¹If an abbot has need of a priest or a deacon, he chooses someone from his own community who is worthy of the ministry and then has him ordained. ²Once he is ordained, he must take heed not to become proud or to become swollen with arrogance. ³He must not dare to do anything that his abbot does not command. Let him also know that, the greater his rank, he must be all the more humble in his submission to the rule.²⁵⁷ ⁴Let him not neglect obedience and the discipline of the holy rule because of the confidence he places in his priesthood. Rather, let him on account of his rank progress ever more and more toward almighty God.

⁵He will hold the same place, corresponding to his entrance into monastic life, ⁶except in his service at the <holy> altar and if it is the abbot's and the entire community's decision to honor and reward the merit of that man's life. ⁷He must realize, however, that he is always subject to the holy rule and to the prior and must do and bear what they rightly teach.²⁵⁸ ⁸If he

---

reading "eius" instead of *RB 1980* 61.12, "eorum" ("their" [my translation]), offering a stark shift in number.

²⁵⁷ "Let . . . rank": expanding upon *RB 1980* 62.3, "sciens se multo magis disciplinae regulari subdendum" ("[he] must recognize that now he will have to subject himself all the more to the discipline of the rule").

²⁵⁸ "He . . . prior": translating *RB 1980* 62.7, "regulam decaniis vel praepositis constitutam sibi servare sciat" ("Yet, he must know how to keep the rule established for deans and priors").

dares to do anything opposed to these in his arrogance, he will not be regarded as a priest but as a rebel <against God>. [9]If after warnings he will not amend, let the bishop be brought in as a witness. [10]If he still will not improve and his sins are evident, let him be dismissed from the monastery—[11]though only if he was so arrogant that he would not submit to and obey the holy rule.[259]

LXIII. Concerning the Community's Proper Order

[1]Rank in the monastery is held and arranged according to the monks' entry into monastic life, the merit of their lives, and the abbot's ordering. [2]The abbot should not disturb or vex the flock subject to him or mismanage anything or order things unjustly, as if he had the freedom to do as he willed. [3]He must know that at God's Judgment he will have to render an account and answer for all his judgments and deeds.[260] [4]According to the order the abbot has established and the brothers hold among themselves,[261] they each give the kiss of peace, go to Communion, stand in choir and sing psalms, <and begin their turns for service>. [5]In no place should rank be determined by age, lest the aged crowd out youth. [6]For Samuel and Daniel were still boys when they judged their priestly elders.[262]* [7]Therefore, except those who on

*1 Sam 3;
Dan 13:44-62

[259] "would not": translating the *receptus* reading "noluerit" instead of *RB 1980* 62.11, "nolit" ("will not").

[260] "He . . . deeds": translating *RB 1980* 63.3, "sed cogitet semper quia de omnibus iudiciis et operibus suis redditurus est Deo rationem" ("He must constantly reflect that he will have to give God an account of all his decisions and actions").

[261] "and": translating *RB 1980* 63.4, "vel" ("or").

[262] "priestly elders": translating *RB 1980* 63.6, "presbyteros" ("elders") as OE *ealdædum mæssepreostum*, drawing on the ambiguous nature of Lat *presbyter*, which can mean both "elder" and "priest."

account of their sins are demoted from their rank or on account of their holiness of life are promoted, everyone else—<the exceedingly old and the young>— should maintain their rank just as they entered monastic life. ⁸And so I say if two turned to God on the same day, the one who came in at the first hour of the day is higher in rank than the one who came in the second hour, whatever his age or dignity.²⁶³ ¹⁰The younger monks must honor their elders, and the elders must love the younger. ¹¹No one should dare to address another by name alone, ¹²but the elders call the younger brother and the younger call their elders *nonnus*—that is, "beloved and honored one."²⁶⁴ ¹³The abbot, who is the vicar of God, is called *lord* and *father*, not on account of his own merits but out of honor for Christ and the love that he proclaims.²⁶⁵ ¹⁴He must always reflect on this and maintain a virtuous way of life, that he might be worthy of such honor.

¹⁵Wherever brothers meet, the younger always requests a blessing from his senior. ¹⁶If an elder passes by where a younger monk is sitting, the younger rises in humility and provides a seat for his elder. The younger should not dare to sit with the elder unless the latter bids him to. ¹⁷In this way they ever observe what is written in the Scriptures—that is, that *they*

---

²⁶³ "And so I say": translating *RB 1980* 63.8, "ut verbi gratia" ("For example"). "turned to God": translating *RB 1980* 63.8, "venerit in monasterio" ("came to the monastery"), as OE *to Gode gecyrrað*. Omitting *RB 1980* 63.9.

²⁶⁴ "that . . . one": translating *RB 1980* 63.12, "quod intellegitur paterna reverentia" ("which is translated as 'venerable father'").

²⁶⁵ "who . . . God": translating the *receptus* and *interpolatus* reading "vices Christi agit" instead of *RB 1980* 63.13, "quia vices Christi creditur agere" ("because we believe that he holds the place of Christ"). "but . . . proclaims": translating *RB 1980* 63.13, "sed honore et amore Christi" ("but out of honor and love for Christ").

*Rom 12:10
should observe honor between them and meet one another with honor.[266]*

¹⁸Small children and youths are kept in rank with discipline and obedience whether in church or at table. ¹⁹They should be supervised with discipline and great care—whether they are inside, outside, or anywhere— until they come to a sensible age and full maturity.[267]

LXIV. Concerning the Election of an Abbot

¹In electing an abbot, the aim—<taken up with the greatest discretion>—should always be to install an abbot who is chosen by the entire community in unanimity and wholeness in accord with the fear of God.[268] If in general council the community provides bad counsel and a few experienced individuals in the community who possess more wisdom recognize what is necessary, their counsel should prevail, since they make their decision with the fear of God and wisdom though they are few.[269] <The others should offer no resistance to the decision.>[270] ²The abbot

[266] *"they should . . . honor"*: translating *RB 1980* 63.17, *"Honore invicem praevenientes"* (*"They should each try to be the first to show respect to the other"*).

[267] *"whether . . . anywhere"*: translating *RB 1980* 63.19, *"Foris autem vel ubiubi"* (*"Outside or anywhere else"*). *"until . . . maturity"*: translating *RB 1980* 63.19, *"usque dum ad intellegibilem aetatem perveniant"* (*"until they are old enough to be responsible"*).

[268] *"taken . . . discretion"*: presumably expanding upon the word *"ratio"* (*"reason"* or *"principle"*) in *RB 1980* 64.1.

[269] *"If . . . few"*: translating *RB 1980* 64.1, *"sive etiam pars quamvis parva congregationis saniore consilio elegerit"* (*"or by some part of the community, no matter how small, which possesses sounder judgment"*).

[270] *"The . . . decision"*: The expansion of the previous line and the stress it lays on the *"few experienced individuals in the community"* along with this complete importation may reflect the reforming tendencies and policies in tenth-century England. When the reformers were refounding monasteries and founding

should be chosen according to the merit of his life and the wisdom of his teaching, even if he was the last to come to the monastery and the lowest in the community's rank.

³If it should happen that the entire community unanimously chooses someone who approves of their sins and goes along with their will—⁴pious and orthodox believers making this known to the bishop in whose diocese the holy place is—⁵[the bishop] must suppress and block the perversity of their evil counsel and with the assistance of other abbots and orthodox believers install and consecrate to the office of the abbacy a man who will set God's house in good order and proceed in God's justice, not in the will of wicked men.²⁷¹ ⁶Both the bishop and orthodox believers

---

new ones along reforming lines, we might assume that the likelihood of the entire community's reliably selecting a superior most in line with the new monastic and royal policies was unlikely. (Or, at least, that the reformers themselves doubted that communities would be able to make such a choice well.)

²⁷¹ "If . . . men": freely translating *RB 1980* 64.3-5, "Quod si etiam omnis congregatio vitiis suis—quod quidem absit—consentientem personam pari consilio elegerit, et vitia ipsa aliquatenus in notitia episcopi ad cuius dioecesim pertinet locus ipse vel ad abbates aut christianos vicinos claruerint, prohibeant pravorum praevalere consensum, sed domui Dei dignum constituant dispensatorem" ("May God forbid that a whole community should conspire to elect a man who goes along with its own evil ways. But if it does, and if the bishop of the diocese or the abbots or Christians in the area come to know of these evil ways to any extent, they must block the success of this wicked conspiracy, and set a worthy steward in charge of God's house"). As in the immediately preceding note and expansions, it may be that the reforming impetus behind the movement of which Æthelwold's translation of the Rule was a part led to a stricter emphasis on the role of discerning authorities (especially the bishop) to ensure that monasteries and their superiors fulfilled the reformers' vision. The lengthy and involved sentences through which Æthelwold has expanded the sentences in the present paragraph rhetorically reflect a particular preoccupation with the administration and maintenance of monasteries

should know that they will receive a great reward
from God if they do this in fear of him. And they will
suffer greatly if they permit these things to occur and
fail to put them right in their negligence.[272]

⁷Once he has been installed, the abbot must consider
how great the burden and how serious the office he
has undertaken are.[273] ⁸He must know and meditate
more upon how he can profit souls, not giving thought
to his own power and dominion. ⁹Indeed, he should
be well versed in divine teaching and in wisdom,
knowing how to interpret the holy narrative of both
the Old Testament and the New.[274] <He should live in

---

through their superiors that is appropriate to his reforming
agenda. Therefore, I have not attempted to simplify Æthelwold's sentence structure and syntax overmuch. For additional
commentary on this particular addition to Æthelwold's Old
English Rule, see Gretsch, *Reform*, 137–38.

[272] "Both . . . negligence": freely translating *RB 1980* 64.6,
"scientes pro hoc se recepturos mercedem bonam, si illud caste
et zelo Dei faciant, sicut e diverso peccatum si neglegant"
("They may be sure that they will receive a generous reward
for this, if they do it with pure motives and zeal for God's honor.
Conversely, they may be equally sure that to neglect to do so is
sinful").

[273] Omitting *RB 1980* 64.8, "et cui *redditurus est rationem vili-
cationis* suae" ("and remember to whom he will have *to give an
account of his stewardship*") (citing Luke 16:2).

[274] "he . . . New": translating *RB 1980* 64.9, "Oportet ergo
eum esse doctum lege divina, ut sciat et sit unde *proferat nova
et vetera*" ("He ought, therefore, to be learned in divine law, so
that he has a treasury of knowledge from which he can *bring
out what is new and what is old*" (citing Matt 13:52). Here, Æthelwold follows Smaragdus, *Expositio* 64.9 (314–15; Comm 504),
in thinking of Benedict's suggestion for knowing "*what is new
and what is old*" in light of scriptural knowledge: "Ac si diceret:
Sit abbas doctus lege divina quae novo et veteri testamento
constat, et ex illa sciat et cognoscat fratribus proferre nova et
vetera testimonia" ("As though to say: The abbot should be
learned in the divine law, which consists of the New and Old
Testament, so that he may know and learn how to bring forth
from it for the brothers new proofs and old").

such a way that others can speak to his holiness>: he should be chaste, temperate, and merciful. [10]*Mercy must always be more powerful than just judgment,** so that he may obtain the same measure of mercy from God.[275] [11]He must hate sins and love the brothers. Let him be wise and thoughtful in his deeds. [12]He should not reprove [the brothers] overzealously, lest he break the rusty vessel by rubbing too hard.[276] [13]He must always consider his own fragility and so be cautious, lest he *crush the bruised reed.** [14]We do not teach with these prudent examples and cautious instruction that he should promote sins and allow them to grow, but rather that he should wisely and with charity diminish them as he sees fit, <so that he can profit his subordinates>, just as we previously said. [15]He must take thought and endeavor that they love him more than they fear him.

*Jas 2:13

*Isa 42:3

[16]He must not be excitable, anxious, extreme, obstinate, envious, or deceitful, for a man <led by vice> is troubled and restless. [17]He should always show forethought and consideration in his orders. In all the work he entrusts [to the brothers], in both divine and worldly matters, he should be discerning and moderate. [18]He should consider the discretion of Saint Jacob the patriarch, who says, *If I press and work my flocks too hard along the way, they will all die in a single*

---

[275] *"Mercy . . . judgment"*: translating *RB 1980* 64.10, "et semper superexaltet misericordiam iudicio" ("He should always *let mercy triumph over judgment"*). "so . . . God": translating *RB 1980* 64.10, "ut idem ipse consequatur" ("so that he too may win mercy"), and drawing on the similarity of measurement mentioned in Matt 7:2, Mark 4:24, and Luke 6:38.

[276] "He . . . hard": translating *RB 1980* 64.12, "In ipsa autem correptione prudenter agat et ne quid nimis, ne dum nimis eradere cupit aeruginem frangatur vas" ("When he must punish them, he should use prudence and avoid extremes; otherwise, by rubbing too hard to remove the rust, he may break the vessel").

*Gen 33:13

day.[277]* [19]Drawing on this and other examples of true discretion, the mother of all virtues, <and practicing moderation in all things>, he should give commands so that the strong have something to desire and the weak do not flee <because of the oppressive nature of their service>.

[20]Indeed, above all else let him be mindful that he observe and fulfill the precepts of this present rule in all its particulars. [21]When he has served well <and zealously defended our Lord's flock, exhorting them rightly>, he will <receive an eternal reward> from the Lord <and happily> hear what that good servant, who gave his fellow servants wheat at the proper time, heard: [22]*Truly I tell you, he sets him as superior over all*
*Matt 24:47
his possessions on account of his conduct.[278]*

LXV. Concerning the Monastery's Prior

[1]Too often the improper appointment of a prior has led to serious contention and discord in monasteries. [2]Some priors, puffed up with the cursed spirit of pride and considering themselves second abbots—<and reckoning themselves virtuous on this account>—are full of contention and great discord and promote diverse disputes in the community.[279] [3]This occurs most often in places where the prior is given his charge by

---

[277] "Saint": the OE *sancte* is a loanword that is used in the Modern English sense of "St." Though Lat "sancti" in *RB 1980* 64.18 is probably best translated "holy" with reference to Benedict's own time, had Æthelwold intended this more general adjective, the OE word would likely have been *halig* ("holy," "set aside for religious use").

[278] "*Truly . . . conduct*": translating *RB 1980* 64.22, "*Amen, dico verbis*, ait, *super omnia bona sua constituit eum*" ("*I tell you solemnly*, he said, *he sets him over all his possessions*").

[279] "are . . . discord": translating *RB 1980* 65.2, "assumentes sibi tyrannidem" ("usurp tyrannical power").

the same bishop or abbots who install the abbot and place him in his office. ⁴It is easy to understand from what grounds this absurdity gives rise to such great pride: ⁵he thinks that he has no need to obey the abbot <since [the abbot] did not appoint him to the office of prior>—⁶rather, he received his office from those who chose the abbot for his own office.²⁸⁰

⁷This stirs up envy and great enmity, contention, slander, rivalry, discord, and disorders. ⁸When the abbot and the prior are in discord and contend between themselves,²⁸¹ they lose their own souls on account of this peril as well as the souls of those subjected to them, ⁹as some of the monks deceitfully attach themselves to one and take his side while others take the other's side.²⁸² ¹⁰The peril of this evil is the responsibility of those in authority who initiated such an arrangement and order.

¹¹We therefore judge and reckon it most profitable for the preservation of peace and charity in the community that the arrangement and ordering of the entire monastery should lie in the abbot's judgment and teaching. ¹²If possible, deans should arrange and order the business of the monastery according to the abbot's

---

²⁸⁰ "he received . . . those": translating the *receptus* and *interpolatus* reading "ab ipsis est ordinatus" instead of *RB 1980* 65.6, "ab ipsis es et tu ordinatus" ("you were made prior by the same men").

²⁸¹ "between themselves": translating the *receptus* and *purus* reading "invicem," which *RB 1980* 65.8 omits.

²⁸² "When . . . other's side": translating *RB 1980* 65.8-9, "ut dum contraria sibi abbas praepositusque sentiunt, et ipsorum necesse est sub hanc dissensionem animas periclitari, et hi qui sub ipsis sunt, dum adulantur partibus, eunt in perditionem" ("with the result that, while abbot and prior pursue conflicting policies, their own souls are inevitably endangered by this discord; and at the same time the monks under them take sides and so go to their ruin").

direction.[283] [13]In this way, the business of the monastery is entrusted to many and no one individual will be led into pride. [14]If the local conditions dictate it and the community desires it with due discretion and humility—and the abbot thinks it wise—[15]then the abbot himself should choose someone with the counsel of God-fearing brothers and install him as prior. [16]The prior must worthily do all that his abbot entrusts to him, doing nothing against his abbot's will and arrangements, [17]for the more honor he is given, the more he must eagerly observe God's directions and the precepts of the rule.

[18]If the prior is found to be sinful, is seduced by pride, or scorns the precepts of the holy rule, he should be warned verbally four times. [19]If he does not amend after verbal admonition, he should be punished according to the teaching of the rule. [20]If he does not correct himself after this discipline, let him be dismissed from the office of prior and another who is worthy put in his place. [21]If after being deprived of his office he is not an agreeable and obedient member of the community, he should be driven out of the monastery completely. [22]Yet the abbot must consider that he will render an account of all his deeds and judgments to <almighty> God and take heed that he not act against the prior in envy, so searing his own soul.[284]

LXVI. Concerning the Monastery's Porter

[1]At the monastery's gate, set a porter who is old and wise, who knows how to deliver a response and receive a message <with discretion>. His consistent

---

[283] Omitting *RB 1980* 65.12, "ut ante disposuimus" ("as we have already established").

[284] Omitting *RB 1980* 65.22, "flamma" ("flames [of jealousy]"), thus rendering the final "so searing his own soul" less powerful as an image.

maturity should be such that he does not wander about, <nor should he enjoy going here and there>. ²The porter must have a cell near the gate so that whoever visits the monastery will always find him ready to retrieve answers <to their messages>. ³When a visitor knocks or a poor person calls out, he immediately says, "Thanks be to God," and readily blesses him.²⁸⁵ ⁴Then, with the gentleness that comes from the fear of God, he promptly gives an answer with the warmth of charity. ⁵If the porter needs help, let one of the younger brothers be entrusted to serve alongside him.

⁶If possible, the monastery should be so constructed that every necessity is contained within it—that is, water, mill, and garden, along with the various crafts that are <good> to practice. ⁷In this way, there will be no need for monks to venture outside, since going abroad is not at all good for their souls.

⁸I desire that this rule be read often in the community so that no one may excuse himself on account of ignorance.²⁸⁶

LXVII. Concerning Those Sent out of the Monastery on an Errand

¹Brothers sent out on account of some need should commend themselves to the common prayer of the abbot and all the [other] brothers. ²While they are gone, they should be remembered and prayed for by the whole community at the end of each canonical hour. ³On the first day that they return home and

---

²⁸⁵ "and readily blesses him": translating *RB 1980* 66.3, "aut Benedic" ("or, 'Your blessing, please'").

²⁸⁶ "I desire": translating *RB 1980* 66.8, "volumus" ("We wish"). "so that . . . of ignorance": cf. Æthelwold's own rationale for translating the rule in "King Edgar's Establishment of Monasteries," Appendix 3, below.

arrive at the monastery, they prostrate themselves in the oratory at the end of each of the canonical hours. [4]Everyone prays together for them, that they will suffer no harm if they sinned on their journey, either by seeing or hearing something evil or through idle talk.

[5]No one should dare to recount to another or make known verbally what he saw or heard outside the monastery, for this greatly dissipates virtue. [6]If someone dares to do so, let him be subjected to proper punishment.[287]

LXVIII. Concerning Impossible Orders

[1]If a brother is unexpectedly commanded to do something burdensome that he cannot do, he receives his superior's order with complete gentleness and great humility.[288] [2]If he then perceives in his obedience that the severity of the order is entirely beyond his powers, he should patiently make this inability known to his superior at an appropriate time.[289] [3]Yet he should not be obstinate, proud, or contradictory. [4]If the superior continues to affirm the order, the younger must know certainly that it is best for him. Trusting in God, he must obey with charity, <though the task be beyond his power>.[290]

---

[287] "proper": translating *RB 1980* 67.6, "regulari" ("of the rule"); omitting *RB 1980* 67.7, "Similiter et qui praesumpserit claustra monasterii egredi vel quocumque ire vel quippiam quamvis parvum sine iussione abbatis facere" ("So too shall anyone who presumes to leave the enclosure of the monastery, or go anywhere, or do anything at all, however small, without the abbot's order").

[288] "great humility": translating *RB 1980* 68.1, "oboedientia" ("obedience").

[289] Omitting *RB 1980* 68.2, "suae causas" ("the reasons why").

[290] "though . . . power": possibly drawing on Smaragdus, Expositio 68.5 (328; Comm 525), where Smaragdus cites Basil

LXIX. Concerning How in the Monastery One May Not Defend Another

[1]Great care must be taken that no brother dare to defend another with words or to protect another at any opportunity, <even if the same thing is said of them both>.[291] [3]In no way should monks presume to do this, for it can lead to the greatest contention and the worst stumbling block of grave discord.[292] [4]If someone disregards this warning and presumes to do so, he should be rebuked most severely.

LXX. Concerning How One Should Not Strike Another

[1]In the monastery every occasion for presumption should be forbidden.[293] [2]We arrange and establish that no one is permitted to excommunicate or strike any brother, unless the abbot has given that monk power

---

as saying, "Omne quod tibi iniunctum fuerit religionis gratia libenter obtempera, etiamsi supra vires tuas fuerit" ("'Willingly comply with everything enjoined on you for religion's sake, even if it is beyond your strength'").

[291] "even . . . both": This is an obscure clause, but it seems to reflect Smaragdus, Expositio 69.1 (329; Comm 526), "Sibi enim quisque timet, cum alium videt corripi. Ideo contra verba corripientium unanimiter surgunt" ("Everyone is afraid for himself when he sees another being rebuked. And so they rise up of one accord against the words of those rebuking them"), and replaces *RB 1980* 69.2, "etiam si qualivis consanguinitatis propinquitate iungantur" ("even if they are related by the closest ties of blood"). For a different interpretation of this passage, which involves emendation, see Gretsch, Reform, 138–40.

[292] "the greatest . . . discord": translating *RB 1980* 69.3, "gravissima occasio scandalorum oriri" ("a most serious source and occasion of contention").

[293] "be forbidden": translating the *receptus* and *interpolatus* reading "vetetur" instead of *RB 1980* 70.1, "vitetur" ("be avoided").

and permission to do so. ³*The sinful should be punished
publicly before the whole community, that the rest might
fear.** ⁴The whole community should reprove the vices
of children and care for them devotedly until they are
fifteen years old, ⁵provided this is done with all moderation and discretion.

*1 Tim 5:20

⁶If someone in his presumption directs and imposes
punishment on someone older, unless this is at the
abbot's behest, let him be subjected to proper punishment. Let those who flare up unreasonably against
children be reproved similarly,²⁹⁴ ⁷for it is written:
*What you do not want done to yourself, do not do to
another.**

*Tob 4:16

LXXI. Concerning Mutual Obedience

¹Obedience is a blessing and a virtue that should
always be given and offered to the abbot <with great
humility>, and not only to him, but each brother
should also graciously obey the others.²⁹⁵ ²They should
know that the way to God is cleared by means of obedience. ³The abbot possesses power through all his
orders and those of the superiors he has appointed.
We permit no other orders to supersede these. ⁴Other-
wise, each obeys the others with charity and great
orderliness. ⁵If anyone is contentious about this, he
should be reproved.

⁶If a brother is reproved or corrected for a little fault
by his abbot or any of his superiors, ⁷or if he perceives

---

²⁹⁴ "If . . . similarly": translating *RB 1980* 70.6, "Nam in for-
tiori aetate qui praesumit aliquatenus . . . vel in ipsis infantibus
sine discretione exarserit, disciplinae regulari subiaceat" ("If a
brother . . . assumes any power over those older or, even in
regard to boys, flares up and treats them unreasonably, he is to
be subjected to the discipline of the rule").

²⁹⁵ Omitting *RB 1980* 71.1, "ab omnibus" ("by all").

that one of them is disturbed by him—even if it is on account of a small or insignificant reason—[8]he should immediately prostrate himself before him without delay and lie stretched out at his feet until his senior gladdens him by offering a blessing. [9]If he scorns this course of action and will not do so, his wickedness should be corrected with blows. If he persists in his pride, he should be completely expelled from the monastery.

LXXII. Concerning the Good Zeal that Monks Should Possess

[1]Just as there is a wicked zeal and emulation of bitterness that separates one from God and leads to hell, [2]so there is a good zeal and emulation that separates one from the vice of sin and leads to God and eternal life. [3]This former zeal then monks should cast aside, while they should eagerly cultivate the latter with the surging flame of charity.[296] [4]*Each must be intent with dignity and longing for divine* life *upon how he may surpass the next in holy service.*[297]* [5]With patience let them bear one another's weaknesses of body and frailty of conduct <and make amends for them>, [6]contending to obey one another <most powerfully>. [7]No one should follow his own judgment concerning what he reckons most profitable and beneficial for himself. Rather, he should do what will most benefit another. [8]They share the peace of brotherhood with one another in charity, [9]ever fearing their Lord [10]and loving their

*Rom 12:10

---

[296] "This . . . charity": translating *RB 1980* 72.3, "Hunc ergo zelum ferventissimo amore exerceant monachi" ("This, then, is the good zeal which monks must foster with fervent love").

[297] "Each . . . service": translating *RB 1980* 72.4, "honore se invicem praeveniant" (*"They should each try to be the first to show respect to the other"*).

abbot with singular and humble love.[298] [11]Let them consider nothing of greater importance or more dear than their Lord, [12]he who will lead us all to eternal life.

LXXIII. Concerning How the Observance of Every Justice Is Not Laid Down in This Rule

[1]We have written this rule, this guide for life, so that by observing it in the monastery we can demonstrate that we have to some extent the beginning of a virtuous way of life and dignity of conduct.[299] [2]For anyone who desires to possess the perfection of a holy way of life, the teachings of the holy Fathers are set forth <as the model of life>, the cultivation and observance of which will lead him to the heights of perfection. [3]Indeed, what page or passage of divine authority found in the Old and New Testaments is not the surest model for our human life? [4]Or which book of the holy and catholic Fathers does not call out and invite us to the true course to our Creator? [5]The lives and conduct of the holy Fathers, the rule of our holy father Basil:[300] [6]what are these if not <the edifice and> the tools of holy men, obedient monks who live well and justly? [7]Yet they make us blush for shame, we who are slothful and live unjustly in wickedness and negligence. [8]Whoever is hastening to approach his heavenly home must begin with God's help and with him fulfill this little rule that we have written as a beginning <of the

[298] "They . . . love": translating *RB 1980* 72.8-10, "caritatem fraternitatis caste impendant, amore Deum timeant, abbatem suum sincera et humili caritate diligant" ("To their fellow monks they show the pure love of brothers; to God, loving fear; to their abbot, unfeigned and humble love").

[299] "monastery": translating *RB 1980* 73.1, "monasteriis" ("monasteries").

[300] Omitting *RB 1980* 73.5, "et Collationes . . . et Instituta" ("the *Conferences* . . . their *Institutes*").

virtuous life>. [9]And then, with God's assistance, you will come to those greater heights of teaching and holy virtues that we have discussed above, <so that you may come to the reward of eternal life and to communion with God and all those who keep this rule>.

<Here Ends the Rule of Our Great Father and Blessed Abbot Benedict, in the Name of God, Christ Our Savior.>

Appendix 1

I. Concerning the Kinds of Monks (BL MS. Cotton Faustina A. x)

As was discussed in the introduction to this volume, all manuscripts of the Old English Rule exhibit signs of being based upon a version intended for women; only one of those manuscripts has not been altered for male use. However, the most significant variants within this divergence among versions are clearly the replacement of two chapters (one and sixty-two) in the Faustina manuscript. What follows below is a translation of the Old English text of chapter one in this manuscript, which is itself largely a translation of Isidore of Seville's *De ecclesiasticis officiis* 2.16. In addition to expanding Benedict's classification of the kinds of monks from four to six and offering further commentary on the differences among them, Isidore's text also discusses aspects of female monastic communities, such as the need to prevent men from visiting in overly familiar fashion.

I follow Schröer's Old English text (134–39). For the Latin text of Isidore's *De Ecclesiasticis Officiis*, see Isidorus Hispalensis, *De ecclesiasticis officiis*, edited by C. M. Lawson, CCSL 113 (Turnholt: Brepols, 1989); for a translation, see Isidore of Seville, *De Ecclesiasticis Officiis*, translated by Thomas L. Knoebel (New York: The Newman Press, 2008).

❖ ❖ ❖

There are six kinds of monks, of which three are the best. The other three are worthless and should be avoided at all cost. The first kind are the cenobites, who pass their common life in a monastery like those saints who followed the apostles, selling all their property or giving it to the poor, and afterward led their lives in common. They did not say that they had anything of their own.* This origin among the apostles and their followers was the beginning of monastic life.

*Acts 4:32

The second kind of monks are the hermits who dwell far from people and live in wastes and deserts and solitary places, imitating Elijah the great prophet and John the Baptist, who inhabited the most isolated places of the desert. Such hermits eagerly despise the world and take pleasure in desert places, living only on plants or bread and water given to them at established times. They live apart, dwelling secretly away from the sight of people, and they frequently enjoy God's own speech, clinging to it with pure minds and rejecting this world and human fellowship.

The third kind are the anchorites, who have been perfected in the monastery and for the love of God shut themselves up in buildings as solitaries, separating themselves from the sight of people. They do not permit anyone to approach them but live only in the contemplation of God.

The fourth kind call themselves anchorites under false pretenses. According to the account of Saint Cassian, they unreasonably consider themselves perfected in the first fervor of monastic life, but they very quickly grow lukewarm and, languishing, continue to cool. They will not renounce their vices and sins, or bear the yoke of humility and patience any longer, or obey the commands of their elders, and so they choose to dwell as anchorites that they may be thought gentle and humble and no one dare challenge them. Those who desire to be anchorites in this fashion will never come to perfection.

With this approach, their vices are not only not weakened but grow much stronger. Their vices are not reformed by others, and so they grow more wicked—just like a lethal poison. As long as one hides this poisonous substance his illness will grow. No one will tell the anchorite of his sins out of respect for him, and so he loves those vices of which he prefers to stay ignorant rather than be cured.

The fifth kind are the wandering vagrants who wander here and there under the guise of a monk, taking with them hypocrisy for sale. They travel on no man's errand, going throughout the various lands, never stable, never staying in one place, never sitting. They feign and relate idle and false accounts concerning what they believe about almighty God. Some possess the limbs of martyrs, but it is doubtful that these are in fact from martyrs. Some enlarge their fringes and phylacteries to obtain idle praise from men.* Some go about with long hair so that the sanctity of the tonsured is not honored more than that of those with long hair. Thus they desire to be compared to Samuel, Elijah, and other holy men, who had long hair.

*Matt 23:5

Some say that they have great honors and powers in their country and they desire to return there. They all beg and ask for assistance for the expense of their sumptuous poverty or the value of their false appearance of holiness. When they are discovered in their wicked deeds and words and are thus found out in some way, their intention is reviled in the name of all monks.

The sixth kind of monk is the worst and most despised, which sprang up at the origin of Christianity among Ananias and Sapphira and was slain by the apostle Peter's rage.* They withdraw from the monastery's customs and follow their own desires. In the Egyptian language they are called *sarabites*, or *renuite*— that is, "those who depend on their own judgment"

*Acts 5:1-11

or "those who deny."[1] They build their own places and call them by the false name of *monastery*. They will not live by the teachings of elders in inferior positions; rather, they follow their own pleasures. They do not do disagreeable work in order to distribute the proceeds to the poor; rather, they pile up the profits and enjoy them themselves. Saint Jerome says that whatever of their labor they sell is more expensive,[2] and so even when their work is holy their lives are not.

Truly, as Jerome himself says concerning them, they fast as a competition and make into a victory what should be done in secret, gaining only arrogance as they make their works known with pomp. They do everything with vanity, having long sleeves and baggy hose, constantly visiting virgins, accusing priests, shunning rough clothing,[3] and indulging until they vomit whenever there is a feast day.

Saint Cassian distinguishes between a *cenobium* and a monastery in this way: the dwelling place of even one monk may be called a monastery; a *cenobium* must be the dwelling place of many. I will make clear the nature of monastic life in the manner our forefathers have done. Certainly, as we said previously, they first forsake this life and its illicit pleasures and observe a holy way of life in common. They lead their lives in holy prayers, readings, disputations, vigils, and fasts. They are not swollen with pride or filled with the venom of envy; rather, they are moderate, cheerful,

---

[1] "*sarabites, or renuite*": Isidore includes the Egyptian word *sarabaitae* followed by the explanation *siue renuite* in Latin. The Old English translator retains both the Egyptian and Latin words, but then duplicates Isidore's explanation in English.

[2] I.e., more expensive than the price set by those in the world.

[3] "shunning rough clothing": This item comes first in the Old English list, but I have moved it in order to prevent the participle from confusing the syntax of the list.

and modest. They live in harmony, making known to one another their thoughts. They deliberate together and set things right.

No one possesses earthly things as his own, and they do not dress in fine or colorful clothing but rather in clothing that is poor and simple. They do not bathe for bodily pleasure but rarely—if infirmity demands it. They go nowhere without the abbot's counsel and do not start anything without the consent of their elders. They work with their hands so that their bodies may be nourished and their minds not be distracted from the Lord. As they work with their hands, they sing psalms and so perform their labor with divine gladness.

Whatever they do, they entrust it to their deans, so that they may be without thought or care for those things that pertain to the body, whether food or clothing or other necessities. The deans entrust these same things to the prior, and the prior disposes and prepares with great care everything necessary on account of the weakness of the body. The prior renders an account to the one they call *father*—that is, the abbot. These fathers must be eminent in intellect, patience, and discretion. Humble and free of pride, they do good to their sons. The authority of the abbots is great in their orders; the willingness of their sons is great in their obedience.

When the signal is given, they frequently gather together in great haste day and night for the canonical hours. They sing the hours with great care of heart until the psalms' end, continuing without weariness. They also gather, fasting, to hear the teaching of their father. They listen to his teaching with great eagerness and great silence, signaling the love of their hearts with moans and weeping as they are brought to recollection by the discourse of the one speaking. They feed their bodies in the great silence only as much as is necessary for maintaining their health. Regarding their eating habits, they restrain the desire of gluttony through abstinence so that their hearts may not be oppressed with poor and unworthy foods.

They certainly abstain from flesh and wine, so that they may restrain all the lusts within them. And not only this, but they abstain from all things that excite powerful desire of mouth and stomach. Whatever they do not consume in their abstinence and whatever remains beyond their needs from what they gain from their labor is distributed to the poor with great care— as much as remains should be given to the poor. To the purpose of this holy service come not only those who are free, but also slaves and others who are the property of other men, the latter very often being freed particularly for this reason.

Rustics and those trained in the various crafts also turn to this same warfare in God's service. Without doubt, they live as monks more easily the more strictly they are raised. If these men are not received [into the community], it is a grave crime. Many of these men have excelled and are imitated only with difficulty, since *God has chosen the weak of the world to shame the strong* who trust in their own strength; *he has chosen the foolish and the despised to reduce to nothing those who consider themselves something, that no flesh may boast before God with pomp.**

*1 Cor 1:27-29

Similarly, there are monasteries where nuns dwell and bear trials, serving our Lord carefully and chastely. Their dwelling is to be kept far apart from the monks, though they are united to these latter in charity, the holiness of religion, and a common search for holy virtues. No young man should visit them, nor mature and proven men, though they may go up to the vestibule if their service requires it. Individual women who are steadfast and proven have power over these communities, their superior positions not only strengthening and preparing their subordinates' conduct but also edifying their minds through teaching and preparation. Preparing woolen clothing for themselves, they also provide the monks with clothing and provide themselves with sustenance. Nuns living in monasteries observe the same conduct, life, and discernment in all things.

Monks are chosen and acceptable to God according to their humility. Many of them are stained by idle praise and seduced by false pride, exalted for their great abstinence and their learning. They do good works for idle praise and not eternal life, desiring the glory of idle praise that they might come in their arrogance to the dignity of their desired honor. Among such monks discord arises. If some brother progresses toward God, the others are envious and love of temporary things prevails. They shamelessly and greedily follow earthly pleasures, often in the sight of others. Those who live this way should not be called monks, for they are not joined to God by virtuous deeds but rather in the words of their confessions alone.

Appendix 2

LXII. Concerning the Monastery's Priests and Their Servants (BL MS. Cotton Faustina A. x)

As is described more fully in the introduction to this volume and the introduction to Appendix 1, the Faustina manuscript of the Old English Rule includes two chapters that are derived from texts other than the Rule of Saint Benedict. The present chapter, replacing chapter sixty-two, comes ultimately from the twenty-seventh chapter of a ninth-century Carolingian text composed in Latin, known as *Institutio sanctimonialium Aquisgranensis*.[1] The text is sometimes attributed to Amalarius of Metz and was intended to govern the conduct of canonesses by the synod convened by Louis the Pious in 816. The present text replaces the chapter concerning the function and conduct of priests in the monastery, offering instead guidelines for how a priest or deacon should visit a (presumably) female community. However, disconcertingly, the changes made to the Old English text in order to make it appropriate for a male community render the sense somewhat awkward. The prime example of this awkwardness is the text's special mention that a priest should not hear

---

[1] An adapted version of this text occurs in Claudius D. iii, for the text of which see Rohini Jayatilaka, *The Old English Benedictine Rule*, 165–66.

confession in private but before others—perhaps good
practice even within male communities, but clearly
more necessary within female communities. Yet the
manuscript's reading has been changed to comment
on the desire of one of the "brothers" to give his confession. Again, such a guideline is not absurd for a
men's community, but one can see it making better
sense in the context of a female community.

I follow Schröer's Old English text (140–41). For the
Latin text of *Institutio sanctimonialium Aquisgranensis*,
see Albert Werminghoff, *Concilia aeui Karolini* I, Monumenta Germaniae Historica, Legem Sectio III Concilia
39B (Hannover: Impensis Bibliafolii Hahniani, 1906),
421–56.

❖ ❖ ❖

If an abbot would like a priest or deacon to come to
the monastery to sing Mass and to perform the venerable services with dignity, he should choose those who
are beyond reproach and deserving of the priesthood
in every desirable virtue. They should yearn after purity, being patient and humble. They should not presume to do anything in the monastery but sing Mass.
They are not to speak with the brothers, nor should
they linger there after Mass has been sung. Rather, as
soon as Mass has been sung, they should depart. The
brothers should readily take heed that they do not
speak with the priest or his servants alone. If one of
the brothers desires to confess his secret sins to the
priest, he should do so in the church with the abbot's
permission rather than in a secret place. They do this
so that other brothers may see them, just as it is commanded by the holy fathers: if someone is sick and
cannot go to the church, he should confess at his home
in the sight of his brothers. If someone presumes—
without need or the abbot's permission—to speak
with [the ministers], publicly or privately, he should

be reproved severely. The abbot should have a priest, deacon, and subdeacon who are so fitting to the task and pleasing to God by their holiness of life that evil report does not follow them on account of any shameful conduct. Rather, the fame of their virtues should honor all those who chose them to celebrate Mass.

Appendix 3

"King Edgar's Establishment of Monasteries"

As is explained in the introduction to this volume, it is widely accepted that this work, found in only one twelfth-century manuscript, London, BL MS. Cotton Faustina A. x, was composed by Æthelwold as a sort of preface for his Old English Rule. Unfortunately, even this one copy is incomplete. After the previous text in the manuscript, several lines are left blank, suggesting that some (but perhaps not much) of the text's beginning is missing. Likewise, there is a gap in the middle of the text that presumably recounted the decay of monasticism in England after its first flowering in the eighth century and that may have discussed the refounding of Glastonbury and Abingdon. The text draws on Bede's *Ecclesiastical History of the English People* for its vision of early monasticism in England and, most interestingly, describes Æthelwold's motivations and intentions for translating the Rule and distributing the text. The present text ends with an exhortation to abbesses warning them against alienating ecclesiastical property, a concern that harkens to the political and social reforms that went hand in hand with the Benedictine Reform's more obvious reform of monastic observance (for which, see the introduction above and sources cited there). Some have taken this explicit mention of abbesses as evidence that the Old English Rule was originally intended for female monastic communities.

For the Old English text, see Dorothy Whitelock's *Councils and Synods with other Documents Relating to the English Church: I, A.D. 871–1204* (Oxford: Clarendon Press, 1981). I have followed Whitelock's translation in some respects but have departed from her strategies in others (e.g., I translate OE *æfæstnes* as "observance" throughout for consistency, whereas Whitelock varies her translations).

❖   ❖   ❖

. . . the world was mercifully filled with the light of the holy faith by the grace of God, who lives in eternity, created everything at once, and, in preordained times, brought each created thing with its natural form to knowledge and clarity. Yet the great Workman, who, wielding his power, governs and moderates all that he has made, did not wish to stop at that. Rather, he earnestly permitted the same light of the full faith to spring up across the ocean, and wonderfully illuminated and celebrated almost the outermost island in the entire world, which was abundantly filled with the English. Truly, that same island, which was in earlier times filled with pagan worship and had been very sorely deluded, served devilish idols. Yet with the help of the acceptable grace of Christ and of Saint Gregory,[1] bishop of the Roman see, [the island] was saved from the darkness of their faithlessness.[2]

Indeed, the aforementioned bishop, by the admonition of the holy grace of God, once began asking some natives about the practices of that island and whether they were Christians. After asking about this he became so greatly inflamed by the torch of charity that he wished to visit and come to a people so glorious

---

[1] Pope Saint Gregory the Great (ca. 540–604).
[2] The following account of the English and Gregory's concern for them is drawn from Bede, HE, 1.23–26 and, especially, 2.1.

and worthy of God, wishing to cleanse them himself
through the teaching and the example of the true faith
and the bath of holy baptism. A prohibition came to
him from all the Romans, which declared that he could
not begin that expedition nor come to that people so
pleasing and acceptable to him. But he found Saint
Augustine[3]—that most trustworthy son of the holy
faith—to act as his representative and sent him here.
In this way, he would eagerly gain for the almighty
Lord a people so suitable and so pleasing to him and
be very zealous in doing so. By means of messengers,
[Gregory] eagerly exhorted and instructed his representative eagerly that he build monasteries to the
praise and honor of Christ and teach and establish for
the servants of God the same customs that the apostles
had practiced with their community at the beginning
of our Christian religion:[4] *there was one heart and one
soul among them, not one of them had his own possessions,
nor even said that he had any, but all things were held in
common.** These very same customs therefore for a
long time progressed and flourished well in the monasteries of the English because of the admonition of
that holy man. But . . .[5]

*Acts 4:32

---

[3] Saint Augustine of Canterbury (d. 604).

[4] Whitelock notes (145 n. 1) that Gregory gave this answer in
response to Augustine's second question in his *Interrogationes*,
which are found in HE 1.27, and that Gregory says nothing there
of monasteries. However, it seems more likely that Æthelwold
here borrows from Gregory's answer to Augustine's first question, in which he recommends that Augustine "ought to institute that manner of life which our fathers followed in the
earliest beginnings of the Church: none of them *said that anything he possessed was his own, but they had all things in common*"
("hanc debet couersationem instituere, quae initio nascentis
ecclesiae finit patribus nostris; in quibus nullus eorum ex his
*quae possidebant aliquid suum esse dicebat, sed errant eis omnia com-
munia*").

[5] Here there is a gap in the manuscript of one or three folios.
The missing material must at least have recounted the decay of
monastic life in England and may have touched on events in

. . . understood and knew [that man, that is, King Edgar] to be a trustworthy steward of his holy churches before he was revealed to people.[6] He therefore gave him manifold and abundant possessions and power. He neither delayed long nor withheld those powers. It was not long until his brother,[7] who through the ignorance of childhood dispersed this kingdom and divided its unity (and also divided the land of the holy churches among rapacious strangers), reached the end of this transitory life.

After his death, Edgar,[8] the aforementioned king, received by God's grace the entire dominion of the English and brought the division of that kingdom to unity once again. He governed everything so prosperously that those who had lived in former times and recalled his ancestors and knew their ancient deeds marveled very greatly, saying in their amazement, "It is a very great miracle of God that all matters in his royal dominion are prosperously subjected to this young king! His forerunners, who were mature in years, very prudent, knowledgeable in their wisdom, and hard to subdue in any conflict, were never able to hold this entire dominion in such tranquil unity—not by fighting or tribute." But it was nothing to marvel at, as if it were a strange thing when almighty God greatly rewards those who promise him good [service] and afterward fulfill that [promise]. Christ the Lord is to be praised very greatly for these things with all gladness of spirit. Truly the almighty Lord, who

---

the life of King Edgar and the founding of Glastonbury and Abingdon Abbeys (see Whitelock, 145 n. 3).

[6] I agree with Whitelock over Thomas Oswald Cockayne (a previous editor of the text) that the presumed subject of the main clause of this sentence is God, while the object is King Edgar.

[7] King Eadwig (ca. 940–959), King Edgar's older brother, and son of King Edmund and Queen Ælfgifu.

[8] King Edgar (943/4–975), son of King Edmund and Queen Ælfgifu.

knows all things, who knows beforehand all that will occur, who knew how beneficent he wished to be, was always very kind to [Edgar] and always discharged every good thing to him beneficently. It was as if the just and honorable Rewarder preached not with words but with deeds and said, "Now that you eagerly defend and advance my name and dominion—that is, my church, which I rightly possess in my distinctive power—as a reward I will celebrate your name and enlarge your kingdom, which you hold under my power, and advance it in prosperity."

Who is there among the English who does not know how he advanced and defended God's kingdom—that is, God's church—with both spiritual and worldly goods and all his strength? Indeed, as soon as he was chosen for his kingdom, he was very mindful of the promise he had made as a young atheling to God and Saint Mary when the abbot had called him to his monastery.[9] As we said previously, in accordance with the admonition of that promise, he was very mindful at the beginning of his reign to advance that place just as he had previously promised in his youth. And he endowed it so greatly with all manner of things that it was neither inferior to nor weaker than very many of those [monasteries] that his ancestors had advanced over a long period. He immediately commanded a great monastery built there in the space of three years. That fact will seem incredible to everyone who has seen that place later on and fails to recall this. [Edgar]

---

[9] In Anglo-Saxon England, an *ætheling* was a "prince of the royal house," its Latin equivalents being *filius regis* and *clito(n)*. See Blackwell s.v. *ætheling*. Presumably this account was found in the manuscript's missing folios (see n. 5 above). If William of Malmesbury's later account in his *Life of Dunstan* is to be trusted, the monastery in question is Abingdon and the abbot Æthelwold himself, for which see William of Malmesbury, *Saints' Lives: Lives of Saints Wulfstan, Dunstan, Patrick, Benignus, and Indract*, edited by Michael Winterbottom (Oxford: Clarendon Press, 2007?).

commanded that same monastery to be finished quickly and to be consecrated to Saint Mary for the praise and honor of God. And he gathered together there a great community of monks so that they should obey God according to the teaching of the holy rule.

Before that time, there was only a small number of monks in a few places who lived according to the correct rule throughout such a great kingdom. In fact, this situation [persisted] in only one place, which is called Glastonbury. Here [Edgar's] father, King Edmund, had first established monks. The previously mentioned abbot was brought from that place and consecrated to the aforementioned monastery that King Edgar had established and supplied with monks. He was very greatly gladdened by the monks' spiritual undertaking and eagerly began to consider first of all how he could rectify his own life with correct observance. It is written in books, "He who intends to begin a good work, let him begin with himself."* After he was set aright himself, he eagerly began to rectify monasteries throughout his entire kingdom and to build up the service of God. This was carried out, by the supportive grace of God, in the following manner: he made continual use of the counsel of his archbishop Dunstan. Through his admonition, [Edgar] considered the salvation of his soul, and not only that, but all the observance and welfare of his dominion. He cleansed the holy places from the foulness of every man, not only in the West Saxon kingdom but also in the land of the Mercians. Indeed, he drove out the canons, who abounded in the aforementioned sins beyond all bounds, and in those greatest places throughout his entire dominion he established monks for the honorable service of Christ the Savior. In some places he also established nuns and entrusted them to his wife, Ælfthryth,[10] that she might help them in

*see Luke 4:23

---

[10] Queen Ælfthryth (d. 999x1001).

all their needs. He himself always considered the welfare of the monks, and he kindly exhorted her to imitate him by being mindful of the nuns in the same way.

He began with an eager investigation to consider and ask about the commands of the holy rule and wished to know for himself the teaching of the rule—which provides the practice of a just life and an honorable will—and the regulations that attract people to the holy virtues. He also wished to know from that rule the wise disposition that is prudently established concerning the right ordering of unfamiliar matters. Because of his desire for this wisdom, he commanded this rule to be translated from Latin into the English language.[11]

Keen and wise men who clearly understand the twofold wisdom—that is, the wisdom of temporal and spiritual things (each of which also has three divisions)—have no need of this English translation. Yet it is necessary for unlearned laymen who, on account of their fear of the torments of hell and of their love of Christ, abandon this miserable life and turn to their Lord and choose the holy service of this rule. [Without the aid of such a translation,] an unconverted layman, in his ignorance and folly, might break the commands of this rule and use the defense that he misbehaved that day because he did not know any better. Therefore I account translation to be a very prudent project. Clearly it cannot matter by which language a person obtains and turns to the true faith; rather, it only matters that he comes to God. Therefore the unlearned natives ought to have knowledge of this holy rule through its exposition in their own language, that they

---

[11] The *Liber eliensis*, edited by E. O. Blake (London: Offices of the Royal Historical Society, 1962), 2.37, reports that Edgar and Ælfthryth offered an estate, Sudbourne, Suffolk, to Æthelwold so he might translate the Rule into English See the introduction, section II.

may serve God the more eagerly and have no defense
that they were compelled by ignorance to misbehave.

Therefore then, I ask my successors with all zeal
and entreat them in the Lord's name that they ever
increase the observance of this holy rule by the grace
of Christ, and, improving it, that they bring it to a
perfect end.[12] No one should presume, by the devil's
admonition or avarice, to reduce God's patrimony in
landed estates or in any other property—or, in ill will,
to seek how it may be so reduced—lest through
poverty and indigence the surging flame of holy observance grow lukewarm and then completely cool.
May such a thing never come to pass! It seems to me
that the observance of this holy rule was reduced in
former times by the plundering of evil men and by
the consent of kings who had little fear of God. Let
this be a great warning to all of us, and let us ask the
Lord that such wretchedness never return to our
observance.

We also instruct abbesses to be profoundly loyal
and devoted to the commands of the holy rule with
all their spirits.[13] And we bid by the command of almighty God that none of them presume in their indis-
cretion to give God's landed estates to her relatives or
to those with secular power—not for wealth nor flat-
tery. Let them consider that they are established as
see John 10:12   God's shepherds, not as thieves. If any of them, deluded by the devil's temptation, be culpable [of such

[12] It has been suggested recently that the final section of this
text, set off by the shift to the first person, may be intended to
speak in King Edgar's own voice. While I do not think this
reading is necessary to make sense of the text, this proposed
shift to the king's voice does lend a greater sense of clarity to
the final section's address. See Pratt, "The Voice of the King."

[13] The final and explicit address to abbesses may point to the
extant copy of the Prologue's having been intended for a
women's monastery, since abbots would have been just as
capable of alienating ecclesiastical property.

a crime] against God or the world, let neither king nor those with secular power be glad on that account, thinking the way open and material given for him to rob God, him who holds those possessions and never sinned. Nor indeed should any earthly king be so greatly undermined by avarice that he will not allow the heavenly King who created him to be entitled to the same due he himself deserves. If any of the king's reeves is culpable before God or others, who would be so indiscreet and foolish that they would deprive the king of his property because his reeve does wrong? Therefore, in the same manner, whatever among the possessions of the churches is given to the eternal Christ ought to stand through eternity. If anyone is so presumptuous as to pervert this, he will be miserably punished in eternal torments. May none of my successors ever merit such wretchedness.

Appendix 4

Ælfric's Homily
On Saint Benedict, Abbot

The most prolific writer of Old English prose was
the Benedictine priest and abbot Ælfric of Eynsham
(ca. 950–ca. 1010). Educated by Æthelwold at the monastic school at Winchester and deeply concerned
about the quality of contemporary religious instruction and clerical knowledge, Ælfric composed two
series of homilies, one series of saints' lives, pastoral
letters for clergy, a Latin grammar in Old English,
translations and paraphrases of Old Testament books,
and other texts throughout his career. As the most
outstanding student of the early Benedictine reformers, Ælfric brought their methods and concerns to a
new generation even as he adapted to new circumstances, especially renewed Viking attacks.

The present homily, composed for Saint Benedict's
deposition on March 21, comes from the second series
of Ælfric's *Catholic Homilies*, composed during his time
as a monk at Cerne Abbas in Dorset in the 990s. While
it appears that Ælfric expected these homilies, arranged according to the liturgical year, to be used both
as preaching texts during Mass and as reading texts
for concerned audiences, most of them are explicitly
presented as texts for preaching throughout. However,
foreshadowing his later series of saints' lives, the current homily is a narrative primarily comprised of a
translation, adaptation, and expansion of the life of

Saint Benedict as described in Saint Gregory the Great's *Dialogues*. In his use of Gregory's work, Ælfric removes the dialogue structure and strips away much of the historical framework that refers to sixth-century Italy. In addition to Gregory's text, there are also a brief description of the saint, some details from the Rule itself, and material from a text that describes the translation of Benedict's relics to the monastery of Fleury.[1] Fittingly enough for a Benedictine abbot, this is the longest piece in the *Catholic Homilies*.

[1] The description of Saint Benedict (translated here as "This blessed man was cheerful in appearance, had white hair, was beautifully formed, and was filled with great love in his mind, such great love that he dwelt in the heavenly homeland though he remained on the earth," p. 177 below) appears to derive from an antiphon for the office(s) of St. Benedict found in later manuscripts, that is, *Erat vir domini Benedictus vultu placido canis decoratus angelicis tantaque circa eum claritas* [or *caritas*] *excreverat ut in terris positus in caelestibus habitaret* (The man of the Lord, Benedict, was of peaceful expression and was adorned in white as the angels, and such light [or charity] grew up around him, that he lived in heaven though he remained on the earth). The CANTUS database lists the antiphon as occurring on Benedict's feast (March 21), his translation (July 11), and the octave of his translation (July 18) (CANTUS, cantusdatabase.org). Though no antiphoners (the liturgical books that contained the antiphons for the various offices) are extant from Anglo-Saxon England, a number of medieval manuscripts from England and the Continent contain the antiphon. The early thirteenth-century antiphoner in Worcester Cathedral Library Ms F. 160 (facsimile edition in *Codex F. 160 de la Bibliotheque de la Cathedrale de Worcester*, Paleographie Musicale 12 [Tournai: Desclee, 1922]), which, though later than our period, was composed for the heirs of Saint Oswald's reformed cathedral chapter, includes the antiphon in the version that Ælfric translates here, with Lat *caritas* instead of *claritas*. The late-thirteenth or early-fourteenth-century breviary of Hyde Abbey, formerly New Minster in Winchester, preserves this antiphon in a truncated form as a response for the second reading of the first nocturn of Matins of St. Benedict's Feast as well as the second reading of the first nocturn of Matins of the Translation (fol. 292ᵛ); see J. B. L. Tolhurst, ed., *The Monastic*

For the Old English text, see Malcolm Godden, ed., *Ælfric's Catholic Homilies: The Second Series* (London: Oxford University Press, 1979), 92–109; for detailed analysis of sources and method, see Malcolm Godden, ed., *Ælfric's Catholic Homilies: Introduction, Commentary, and Glossary* (Oxford: Oxford University Press, 2000), 429–48.

❖   ❖   ❖

On this present day, the holy abbot Benedict departed from this mortal life to eternal life, which he fully merited by the holiness of his life here. He was nobly born to pious parents, who sent him to Rome as a child to learn from learned philosophers. When he had grown in wisdom, he began to shun the vices of worldly people. He secretly fled that city, and his foster mother followed him. They came to the place called Affile, and pious men detained him there for a time.

His foster mother obtained a sieve, and it broke in two while she had it. She wept sorely on account of the broken item, but the pious Benedict took pity on his foster mother's affliction in his kindness and took the pieces of the split sieve. He knelt in prayer weeping, and when he arose from those prayers he found the vessel lying next to him so whole that there was no crack to be seen. This miracle was immediately made known throughout that area, and the people hung that sieve up at the church gate as a wonder. In

---

Breviary of Hyde Abbey, Winchester, vols. 3 and 4. Later versions of the antiphon read Lat *moribus* for *canis*, the latter of which Ælfric also clearly translates here. I thank Sr. Mary Thomas Brown of St. Cecilia's Abbey (Isle of Wight) for bringing this source to my attention. Though I was not able to do an exhaustive study of the sources for this antiphon before publication, it appears that Ælfric's translation here is the earliest evidence for knowledge of this antiphon in England.

this way, everyone would know the glorious acts of the great Benedict and the honor he possessed before God even as a child.

But Benedict longed more to suffer hardships and toil for God than he cared for worldly praise or the fame this life affords. And so he secretly fled from his foster mother to a wild place called Subiaco forty miles from Rome. There a pious monk named Romanus fed him for three years and clothed him in the monastic habit. Because Romanus could not reach Benedict on account of the cliff, he hung a little bell on that cliff so Benedict could hear—at the bell's ringing—when he should come get his food. Then one day the malicious devil, who was jealous of the monk's charity and his friend's willingness to nourish him, threw a stone at the bell, breaking it apart. But the noble monk did not cease from bringing his friend food at the proper times.

After this, almighty God made holy Benedict known to an honorable priest, and this priest sought him out with gifts at Eastertide, as he had been commanded. He found Benedict on holy Easter in a cave and spoke with him. He then became known widely among the herdsmen, and his name spread everywhere. A great many of them visited him and brought him bodily food, and he gave them food for their souls by his mouth's heavenly teaching.

One day when he was alone, the tempter came to him. A blackbird fluttered about his face so persistently that he could have seized it with his hands if had wanted to. But he blessed himself with the sign of the cross, and the bird immediately departed. Then such a bodily temptation afflicted him that he could hardly withstand the fervor in his body. He considered what to do and then unclothed himself completely and rolled about in some dense brambles, thorns, and nettles, all of which grew thickly there in the wilderness. He did this so long that when he arose he was

heavily scratched, the wounds of his skin extinguish-
ing the wounds of his mind as he turned that sinful
desire into pain and quenched the inner excitement
by means of the outer. Indeed, he overcame sin by
changing the nature of his fervor. Truly, from that time
on, as he himself said afterward, every lustful inclina-
tion was completely eliminated and he never had a
similar feeling again.

Nearby there was a monastery, the abbot of which
had recently died. The monks of this place came to the
holy Benedict with singular purpose and asked him to
become their abbot. He refused for a long time, saying
that their customs would not be in accord with his
disposition. But when they persisted single-mindedly
in their request he finally granted it and established a
regular way of life in their monastery.

Then they saw that their wickedness stumbled upon
the rule of his righteousness, for he would not allow
them to continue in their unlawful ways as they had
previously done. They began to quarrel, among themselves at first, that they had requested his superiority
over them. And finally they decided that they would
kill him with poison. They mingled poison with his
drink, and the servant then stood a distance off with
a glass vessel that held the drink of wine mixed with
the deadly poison. The servant then, according to the
custom of the monastery, bowed with the vessel for
Benedict's blessing. From his seat, he blessed the
vessel with the sign of the cross, and immediately the
vessel burst apart, as if instead of the sign of the cross
he had thrown a stone at it. Then the holy man perceived that the drink was poisoned, since it could not
bear the sign of life. He immediately arose and spoke
to the brothers with a cheerful spirit: "May almighty
God be merciful to you brothers. Why would you give
me this? Did I not tell you before that we would not
be in accord? Go now and seek a superior according
to your own customs, for you cannot have me any

longer." And then he returned to the wilderness and tended to himself.

Very many people then flowed to him, gathering for almighty God's service and living according to his instruction. And so he built twelve monasteries in that place with Christ's help, placing twelve monks within each and retaining a few. The nobly born in Rome started entrusting their children to him for divine instruction. One of these children was called Placid and another Maur. Once Placid had to fetch water at the river, and he fell over the bank into the stream. The holy man Benedict knew that the child was in great danger through the Spirit of God, and he said to Maur, "Brother Maur, run quickly, for the stream is carrying Placid away." Maur immediately sought his blessing and ran, without realizing it, upon the steam as if he were running on solid earth. He grabbed the child by the hair, running with a swift course to the land. Then he realized that he had run upon the water, and he marveled greatly. He told his teacher what had happened, and Benedict said that it had happened through God's power on account of his obedience. Maur said that it had happened because of Benedict's command, while the child Placid said that he saw Benedict's cowl above his head, and it seemed that the cowl had pulled him from the stream.

A monk was irregular in the Divine Office, and he would not attend to the canonical hours with his brothers. Rather, he went out rambling. Then the holy man Benedict saw that the devil, in the form of a black child, drew the monk out by the hem of his garment. On another day, Benedict found this monk away from the canonical hour and struck him with his rod on account of the blindness of his heart. The fiend could not lead him away from the church after this, as if he himself had been struck by Benedict's rod.

Of the twelve monasteries he established, three were set upon high mountains, and the brothers had great danger in climbing down to the cliffs every day to retrieve water. They came to the holy man asking him to build monasteries closer to the water source. He comforted them gently and that same night climbed up the mountain with Placid, the child we spoke of earlier. He lay there a long time in prayer and marked the place. He went back to the monastery in secret and commanded the brothers to dig a small pit where he had marked, saying that almighty God could draw out water from the mountain's summit and relieve them of their labor. Then, at his command, the brothers went to the place he had marked and found a rock that had been sweating. When they hollowed it somewhat, immediately water flowed out so abundantly that it ran like a stream off the mountain, and it has not yet ceased in its abundance.

Once a scythe fell off its handle into a deep pit. Then Benedict arrived and desired to comfort the laborer who had lost the tool. He held the handle above the water where the iron tool had sunk, and immediately it came swimming toward the handle and the hole out of which it had previously fallen.

There was a priest named Florentius in that neighborhood, and he was filled with hatred for the holy man. He wanted to have the fame that Benedict possessed but did not want to live in such a praiseworthy manner. And so he planned to kill Benedict with poison and sent him a loaf of bread as a gift. But the loaf was mixed with poison. Now there was a wild raven who flew daily from the wood to the monastery to receive his food from Benedict's hand. He threw the poisoned loaf to the raven and ordered him in God's name to bear the deadly loaf away to a place where no one would find it. The bird obeyed his command and hastened to the wood with the loaf. After about three hours, he came back to fetch his food, as was his custom.

When the priest perceived that he could not bodily kill the holy man, he longed to destroy the souls of his disciples instead. And so he had seven naked women go in and play in their sight, that their minds might be incited to lust by the play of those shameless women. When the holy man saw the hostile envy of that dishonorable priest, he left the place with his brothers, lest any of his disciples perish because of the priest's jealousy. The priest then stood on the upper floor of his home rejoicing greatly at the other's departure, but the flooring under his feet broke and he died terribly. The house continued soundly except for that one place, which had crushed God's enemy. After Maur asked what had happened to the priest, he said cheerfully to his teacher, "We can return, for the priest who had persecuted you is dead." Benedict lamented with grievous lamentations that his disciple Maur would rejoice at the other's death and gave him a penance, commanding him not to rejoice in his enemy's death.

Benedict then went to the mountain called Cassino, which rises up to a height of three miles. An idol called Apollo was worshipped there for a long time. The holy man overturned that idol from its foundation and erected a church to the honor of Saint Martin as well as an oratory to the praise of Saint John the Baptist, converting the heathen people there to the faith of Christ with constant preaching. The old devil could not endure those acts in silence, and so he appeared before the holy man's sight in a terrible form with a burning mouth and flaming eyes, raging toward him. With a loud cry he lamented his lot, and the brothers readily heard the devilish voice. Then he called him by name: "Benedict"—that is, "Blessed." The holy man remained silent, and the devil immediately called again: "Maledict, not Benedict, you accursed and not blessed man—why do you torture me? Why do you persecute me?"

There was a huge stone among the buildings there, which the laborers wished to raise and use in their building, but they could not lift it since the invisible devil sat upon it. The laborers called out to the holy man, and he came straight away. At his prayers the devil fled. Benedict then gave his blessing, and the laborers moved it as easily as if it had had no weight at all. The holy man then ordered them to dig where the stone had lain, and they found there a brazen image that the devil had protected. They cast the image into the kitchen, and it seemed to them all that a fire came out of the image and was burning the entire kitchen. But it was not as it seemed to them, for it was a delusion sent by the devil. They ran to it, stupefied, and sought to put out the fire with water. The holy man arrived and saw how the accursed spirit deceived them and knelt immediately in prayer. He did this so that the brothers, who were busy with the illusory fire, might see that the kitchen actually stood whole before their sight.

One day the blessed Benedict stood at prayer, while the brothers had gone to work on the wall [they were building]. The devil appeared before the holy man and said tauntingly that he would also go to the worksite. At this, Benedict quickly sent word to warn the brothers of the devil's arrival, but before the messenger could get to the brothers the devil threw down the wall and so crushed a small boy of the community. Benedict ordered them to carry the crushed limbs of the boy to the oratory on a blanket. There he closed the door and lay single-mindedly in prayer until the crushed child revived through God's power: this was indeed a wonderful thing. Then the holy man sent the boy, sound in all his limbs, to the worksite—the very one whose death the devil had desired to use to insult the holy man.

The holy man Benedict progressed in the gift of prophecy, so that through the Spirit of God he could know the future and see things in prophecy that would happen after he died. It was customary in his monastery that brothers going out on an errand would not, without his permission, take food if they could return to the monastery on the same day.[2] One day, two brothers went to get something for the monastery and broke this rule by eating with a pious woman without permission and then returning to the monastery. The holy man asked them in what inn they had tasted food, and they said that they had not eaten any food on their trip. Then the holy man named the pious woman who had invited them, noted the dishes she had given them, and also explained accurately when they had drunk. They fell at his feet in fear, acknowledging their guilt and asking for his mercy.

At that time there ruled a cruel king named Totila. He went to the holy man's monastery one day and sent a messenger to announce his visit to the holy man. The bloodthirsty man wanted to discover whether or not Benedict possessed the spirit of prophecy, so he sent his sword bearer, Riggo, dressed in his royal clothing and accompanied by his servants, to the monastery as if it were the king himself. Then Benedict sat before Riggo, who had entered with false pomp and excessive strutting. The blessed servant of God called out to him, saying, "My son, take off those clothes you're wearing; they are not yours." Riggo prostrated himself upon the ground along with all his companions, deeply frightened that they had dared to put him to the test. They returned to their lord in fear, explaining how quickly they had been found out. Totila himself then went to the monastery, and as soon as he saw the holy man sitting a way off, he prostrated himself upon the ground before him. Benedict ordered him to rise, but he would not dare to stand upon his feet before the holy man. The holy man went to the prostrate king and picked him up, verbally reproving him

---

[2] Ælfric significantly alters the details of the story in this paragraph, apparently in part to accord with RB 51.1-2.

for his works. He also told him truly, by means of prophecy, what would happen in his life. He said, "You do many evil things, and you have done many as well. Put off entirely these unrighteous ways! Indeed, you will go to Rome, you will sail over the sea, nine years you will reign, and in the tenth year you will die." The king was sorely afraid on account of the prophecy and asked for his blessing. From that time on he ceased from his cruelty in part. It happened as the holy one prophesied, and in the tenth year he lost his kingdom and his life.

At the same time, a priest in the church of Aquino went mad and went to blessed Benedict. With holy prayers he drove the devil from the possessed priest and spoke these words to him: "Go now, and from this day forward do not approach God's services, nor eat meat. If you ever dare to approach God's services, you will again be given over to the power of the devil." The priest observed this order for a long time but at last disregarded the holy man's command and foolishly undertook a holy office. Then the devil, who had been unwillingly driven out of him, immediately seized him and tormented him until his death.

A pious person had a boy take the holy man two bottles of wine as a gift. The boy hid one along the way and brought the other to the holy man. He received the gift graciously and said to the boy, "My child, be careful that you do not drink from the bottle that you hid along the way, but tilt it carefully. You will see then what is hidden within." He returned in shame and tilted the bottle carefully. Out of that vessel came a deadly snake.

The holy man said many things in holy prophecy, the extent of which would be too long to recount and for you to hear in this short span of time.

A nobly born child held a light before his table and began to grow proud that he had to serve him in such insignificant matters. The holy man then perceived his pride through the Spirit of God and, severely reproving him, said, "Brother, bless your heart." Then he ordered the light to be taken away from him, had the boy sit down, and then told his brothers all about the child's pride.

One time, a terrible famine came upon the region and greatly afflicted the inhabitants there. Such poverty came upon Benedict's monastery that the brothers only had five loaves left for all of them. With kind words, the holy man Benedict assuaged the brothers' sadness, saying, "Today we have but little, but tomorrow we will have abundance." In the morning they found before their doors two hundred bushels of meal in sacks, which almighty God sent to his servants. But no man knew how they had gotten there.

A pious thane asked the holy man and his monks to build a monastery on his land. Benedict gladly agreed and told his brothers that he would come himself on a particular day to direct the construction of the monastery. The monks then went to the thane's land at his command and, with his blessing, eagerly awaited the appointed day. The holy man Benedict then appeared in a dream to the monk whom he had set over the monastery as well as the prior. On this night before the appointed day, he directed them in great detail concerning the construction of that monastery. When the head monk and the prior awoke they immediately related to one another what they had seen in their dreams and greatly marveled at this. After the appointed day, and the holy man had still not arrived as he had said he would, they went back to him, saying, "We waited for you, holy father, to hear how you would direct us to build the monastery. But you did not come as you had promised." The saint answered them, saying, "My brothers, why do you say that I did not come? Did I not appear to you both in your sleep and teach you clearly concerning the entire building? Go now and build the monastery just as I directed you in your dreams." They went back to that land greatly amazed, and they arranged the construction just as they had seen it in their dreams.

Now holy Gregory, who wrote this account in Latin, says that almighty God—who once swiftly brought the prophet Habakkuk physically from Judea to the kingdom of the Chaldeans so he might provide the hungry Daniel, who though innocent had been placed among the lions, with bodily sustenance*—permitted his beloved Benedict to go to the sleeping brothers in spirit and direct them in the spiritual life.

*Dan 14:32-38

Two monks of noble family lived in the neighborhood of his monastery, both of whom were tended to in worldly concerns by a pious man. On account of the nobility of their birth they were proud and inclined to malicious speech, frequently afflicting the noble man. This pious man told the blessed Benedict about the great injury he had suffered from those monks. The holy man sent a message to them, saying, "Correct your tongues. If you do not do so, I will excommunicate you." But they persisted in their harmful words and died suddenly, being buried in the church. It was customary at Mass in those days, before communion began, for the deacon to call out, "If anyone is unworthy to receive communion, let him leave the church." Those excommunicated monks were buried within the church, as we previously said, and they arose from their graves in the sight of everyone there, obeying the deacon's command since they were cut off from the holy Eucharist. And so it happened at every Mass—they could not remain inside the church at communion once the deacon had given his order. This was made known to holy Benedict, and it caused him great sorrow. Benedict immediately sent for a host and commanded that a Mass be celebrated for the monks with it, saying that they would no longer be excommunicated afterward. His command was fulfilled, and afterward those monks were never seen leaving the church after the deacon's order again. This came about because they had received holy communion from God through his servant, Benedict, who had previously threatened to excommunicate them for their foolish words.

In his monastery lived a monastic child who possessed great love for his father and mother. He became afflicted with a greater longing for his parents than for God's portion and left the monastery without a blessing to go to them. And on that same day he departed from this present life. When he was buried, the grave could not hold him. Rather, his body was found the next day upon his grave. His parents buried him again, and again he was cast back up, and this happened repeatedly. With great weeping, the child's parents sought out the feet of the holy man, requesting his grace. The holy Benedict gave them the divine Eucharist with his own hands and said, "Lay this holy eucharistic bread upon his breast and bury him with it." When they did this, the earth held the child's body and did not cast him out again.

Another monk lacked stability and desired with persistent prayers to leave monastic life. But the holy man forbade it and reproved him verbally for his instability. Finally, since he was so eager to depart, the holy man became angry at his restlessness and bade him go away. The monk left and immediately came upon a dragon whose gaping mouth was ready to swallow him. The monk, trembling and fearing, cried out, "Run! Run! This dragon will swallow me!" The monks there came running to him and saw no dragon at all, for it was the invisible devil. But they led the trembling monk inside the monastery. He immediately promised never to leave the monastery again, and he ever persisted in that promise. Benedict's prayers had made the dragon—whom the monk had previously followed without seeing—visible.

Benedict also healed a boy with great speed, through his prayers, of the terrible illness called *elephantinus morbus*.

A poor man had to pay another man half a pound, and he was frequently reminded and severely afflicted on account of the loan. He asked the holy man for money, and Benedict comforted him in his poverty with kind words. He explained that he did not have any money to lend, but he told the man to come back to see him in three days. Then, as was his custom, he set himself to prayer for the space of those three days. The poor man returned on the third day and found the money and twenty pennies as well upon a box of grain. The blessed Benedict ordered the half-pound owed on the poor man's loan to be given to him and let him keep the twenty pennies for his own needs.

A man was given poison, but it could not kill him. Rather, it covered his skin with a strange eruption so his body looked like that of a man with leprosy. He came to the holy Benedict, and as soon as he touched the saint he regained his health and the eruption disappeared.

A subdeacon asked the holy man for some oil, since in that country they eat oil with their food just as we use butter.[3] Now the holy man had distributed the monastery's goods to the poor during the famine so graciously that there was no oil left for the brothers except that which remained in one little glass vessel. He ordered the cellarer to give the glass vessel to the subdeacon, but the cellarer said in response that if he gave the subdeacon the oil he would have none left for the brothers. The holy man became troubled at this and ordered another monk to throw out the glass vessel with the oil too, lest it should stay there through disobedience. This brother threw the glass vessel out the window onto the hard stone outside, but it did not

---

[3] "since . . . butter": this is, of course, one instance in which Ælfric puts his own commentary explicitly into Gregory's narrative and also gives a rare glimpse into an early medieval monk's comparison of everyday cultural phenomena.

break, nor did the oil spill. Benedict ordered that the oil vessel be picked up and given to the subdeacon who had previously requested it and severely rebuked the disobedient cellarer. Then he knelt at prayer with his fellow monks. Among them was an empty cask that was covered, and it began to flow with oil. So they removed the cloth and the oil flowed over onto the floor. Benedict rose from prayer and the oil stopped flowing.

One day the holy man went to church and encountered the devil. He asked where the devil was going, and [the devil] said he was bringing the brothers something to drink. The holy man quickly started to pray and turned back. Just then, the accursed spirit came upon an old monk drawing water and threw him to the ground, afflicting him terribly with madness. The blessed Benedict struck the monk under his cheekbone with one hand, and the foul devil immediately departed from him, never daring to approach him again.

At that time a heretic named Zalla persecuted Christians with severe ferocity, in such a way that if a priest or a monk came near him he might not escape Zalla's hands alive. Once he seized a Christian man and afflicted him with various torments. In his burning greed, he sought to use those torments to extort the man's property. The Christian then said that he had entrusted his goods and himself to the holy man Benedict. The bloodthirsty persecutor Zalla ceased tormenting him and bound the man with sturdy bonds. As he rode [on a horse], he drove the man before him so that he might see who this Benedict—who had received the man's property—was. They came to the gate of the holy man's monastery and found him sitting there reading. The bloodthirsty Zalla said to the holy man with great ferocity, "Stand up, stand up, and give me this churl's property." Then the holy man looked up at Zalla's calling out and saw the bound man, and at that glance his bonds were loosed with quickness beyond words. Then Zalla became afraid at that great power and bowed his bloodthirsty neck at the holy man's feet, begging for his mercy and intercession. Benedict, however, did not stand up from his reading but ordered his brothers to lead him into the church and give him a blessing. After the blessing, the blessed Benedict urged the cruel persecutor to leave off his mad cruelty. At that he hastened away in great amazement and dared not take anything from that Christian, whom the blessed Benedict had loosed from his bonds—not with his hands but with his gaze.

A faithful plowman brought his dead son's body to Benedict's monastery and, weeping sorrowfully, cried to the holy man, "Give me my son! Give me my son!" The holy man answered, "What, did I take your son from you?" The plowman responded, "Sir, he is dead. Go and raise him." The blessed man said to his brothers, "Go away; this is not our deed, but that of the holy apostles." But the churl continued in his prayer, swearing that he would not depart unless the saint raised his son. Then Benedict went to the boy's body and lay upon it. He rose, stretched out his palms to heaven, and said, "My Lord, do not look upon my sins but on the faith of this man who asks you to raise his son. Give back, O Lord, the soul that you took from this body." Immediately after this prayer, the dead boy came back to life, and the holy man gave him back to his father whole.

The holy man had a pious sister named Scholastica, who was from childhood consecrated to God and served him in virginity. She dwelt near [Benedict's] monastery, and the holy man always visited her once in the course of a year. One day, as was his custom, he came to her cell with some of his brothers. They spent the day in God's praise and holy conversation. But when evening came and they sat to eat, the holy woman said to her venerable brother, "Brother, please do not leave me tonight, that we might discuss the joys of heavenly life until morning." But her venerable brother replied, "What are you saying, sister? I cannot spend the night away from the monastery." There was such still weather that not a cloud was seen in the sky. But when the nun heard her brother's answer, she covered her face with her hands and lowered her head to the table, praying to the almighty Lord. Then, once she raised her head from the table, terrible thunder and lightning burst forth and such a surging storm began that the holy man and his brothers could not, on account of the downpour, move their feet from her cell. The holy man said to his sister, "May almighty God spare you, sister—what have you done?" She answered, "I asked you, and you would not grant my request; I asked my Lord, and he heard me. Go to your monastery now and leave me if you can." He could not leave from under her roof, but had to stay there that night though he did not want to. And all that night they stayed awake, occupied with holy conversation about the spiritual life. Then after three days, the holy man was standing at his prayers and, looking out, saw the soul of the same nun, his sister, being led to heaven in the form of a dove. Rejoicing in her glory, he gave thanks to almighty God and made her death known to his brothers. Immediately, he sent them off to bring her body to the monastery and bury it with honor in his own tomb—where he himself desired to lie—so that their bodies might rest in the same tomb, just as their minds had ever served God in unity.

Another time, the holy man stood at his prayers in an upper story where his bed was. He stood at a window throughout the night, praying to almighty God. Suddenly there appeared a great light, brighter than any day, in which the holy man saw over the entire world and saw among the great beams of light a troop of angels leading the soul of a bishop named Germanus to heaven. The saint wanted witnesses of that wondrous vision and called for his deacon, who quickly came to him and saw a portion of that light. Then the holy man sent a swift messenger to that bishop's city to see whether or not he was alive. The messenger found him there dead and searchingly inquired about his death. He learned that [the bishop] had departed at the very time that the holy Benedict had seen his soul journeying to heaven.

It is a wondrous vision, that a mortal man might see over all the world, though, if a person sees God's light, then creation will seem very narrow to him. And that person's soul will, in God, be expanded through that light so that it will rise above the world and itself as well. What should we consider miraculous in this event, though the holy man saw all the world before him, since he was lifted up above the world in the light of his mind? Certainly the light he saw without was shining within his mind, and it drew his mind to heaven, revealing to him how narrow all the lower creation appeared to him in the immensity of the divine light.

This blessed man Benedict wrote a rule for monks using great discretion and clear language. In it everyone may learn all the aspects of his instruction, for the saint lived as he taught. This blessed man was cheerful in appearance, had white hair, was beautifully formed, and was filled with great love in his mind, such great love that he dwelt in the heavenly homeland though he remained on the earth.

The year that he departed he made known his death beforehand to some of his disciples who lived with him and to some who lived in far-off places. Seven nights before he was to depart he ordered his tomb opened, and at that moment a severe fever greatly afflicted him throughout the next seven days. On the sixth day of his illness, he ordered them to carry him into the church and to give him communion. After this, he stood between his brothers as they supported him, his hands stretched out to heaven and breathing out his spirit among his prayers. On that same day, there appeared to two of his disciples a road that stretched from the building from which he departed—on the eastern side—out to heaven. This road was paved with palls and shone with innumerable lamps. Upon the road stood a venerable man with shining garments, asking what road this was that they saw. They replied that they did not know. Then the angel said to them, "This is the road upon which God's beloved, Benedict, rose to heaven."

His holy body was buried alongside the body of his sister Scholastica, just as he himself had commanded, in the church of John the holy Baptist upon Monte Cassino. But many years later he was taken to the kingdom of the Franks, to the monastery that we call Fleury. There his bones rest in great honor, shining with miracles, and his soul reigns with God in heaven, forever blessed on account of his good merits. The cave in which he first lived also continues up to the present day to shine with miracles. Indeed, once a mad woman went roaming through the woods and fields and lay down where exhaustion stopped her. Then one day she entered Benedict's cave, ignorant of what it was. She rested there and rose in the morning so sound in mind that it was as if she had never been mad at all, continuing this way ever after.

Who on earth can speak of all the wonders that the almighty Creator has revealed throughout the world through this noble man? May glory and praise ever throughout eternity be to him who alone is the inexpressible God, along with all his saints. Amen.

Bibliography

I. Primary Sources

Ælfric of Eynsham. *Ælfric's Catholic Homilies: Introduction, Commentary, and Glossary*. Edited by Malcolm Godden. Oxford: Oxford University Press, 2000.

———. *Ælfric's Catholic Homilies: The Second Series*. Edited by Malcolm Godden. London: Oxford University Press, 1979.

———. *Ælfric's Letter to the Monks of Eynsham*. Edited by Christopher A. Jones. Cambridge: Cambridge University Press, 2009.

Bede. *The Ecclesiastical History of the English People*. Edited and translated by Bertram Colgrave and R. A. B. Mynors. Oxford: Clarendon Press, 1969.

Fairweather, Janet, trans. *Liber Eliensis: A History of the Isle of Ely from the Seventh Century to the Twelfth*. Woodbridge: Boydell and Brewer, 2005.

Gregory. *Moralia in Iob*. Edited by Marcus Adriaen. Corpus Christianorum, Series Latina 143, 143A, 143B. Turnhout: Brepols Publishers, 2005.

———. *Moral Reflections on the Book of Job*. 6 vols. Translated by Brian Kerns. CS 249, 257, 258, 259, 260, 261. Collegeville, MN: Cistercian Publications, 2015–2017. Vols. 5 and 6 forthcoming.

———. *Pastoral Care*. Ancient Christian Writers 2. Translated by Henry Davis. Mahwah, NJ: Paulist Press, 1978.

———. *Regula Pastoralis (Pastoral Care)*. Edited by Guiseppe Cremascoli. Rome: Città nuova, 2008.

Isidore of Seville. *De Ecclesiasticis Officiis*. Translated by Thomas L. Knoebel. New York: The Newman Press, 2008.

Isidorus Hispalensis. *De ecclesiasticis officiis*. Edited by C. M. Lawson. CCSL 113. Turnholt: Brepols, 1989.

Kuhn, Sherman M., ed. *The Vespasian Psalter*. Ann Arbor: The University of Michigan Press, 1965.

Martyrologium Romanum: ex decreto sacrosancti oecumenici Concilii Vaticani II instauratum auctoritate Ioannis Pauli PP. II promulgatum. Editio Typica. Vatican City: Libreria Editrice Vaticana, 2001.

RB 1980: The Rule of St. Benedict in Latin and English with Notes. Edited by Timothy Fry. Collegeville, MN: Liturgical Press, 1981.

Schröer, Arnold, ed. *Die angelsächsischen Prosabearbeitungen der Benediktinerregel.* 2nd ed. rev. by Helmut Gneuss. Darmstadt: Wissenschaftliche Buchgesellschaft, 1964.

Smaragdus of St. Mihiel. *Commentaria in regulam sancti Benedicti: Commentary on the Rule of St. Benedict.* Translated by David Barry. CS 212. Kalamazoo, MI: Cistercian Publications, 2007.

———. *Smaragdi abbatis Expositio in Regulam S. Benedicti.* Edited by K. Hallinger, et al. Corpus consuetudinum monasticarum 8. Sieburg, Germany: F. Schmitt, 1974.

Tolhurst, J. B. L., ed. *The Monastic Breviary of Hyde Abbey.* 6 vols. London: Henry Bradshaw Society, 1932–1942.

Whitelock, Dorothy, ed. *Councils and Synods with other Documents Relating to the English Church: I, A.D. 871–1204.* Oxford: Clarendon Press, 1981.

William of Malmesbury. *Saints' Lives: Lives of Saints Wulfstan, Dunstan, Patrick, Benignus, and Indract.* Edited by Michael Winterbottom. Oxford: Clarendon Press, 2002.

Wulfstan of Winchester. *The Life of St. Æthelwold.* Edited by Michael Lapidge and Michael Winterbottom. Oxford: Clarendon Press, 1991.

II. Secondary Sources

Barrow, Julia. "The Chronology of the Benedictine 'Reform.'" In *Edgar, King of the English 959–975: New Interpretations,* edited by Donald Scragg. Rochester, NY: Boydell and Brewer, 2008. 211–23.

———. "The Ideology of the Tenth-Century English Benedictine 'Reform.'" In *Challenging the Boundaries of Medieval History: The Legacy of Timothy Reuter,* edited by Patricia Skinner. Turnhout: Brepols, 2009. 141–54.

Bately, Janet. *The Literary Prose of King Alfred's Reign: Translation or Transformation?* London: University of London King's College, 1980.

Billett, Jesse D. *The Divine Office in Anglo-Saxon England 597–c. 1000.* London: Henry Bradshaw Society, 2014.

Blackwell Encyclopedia of Anglo-Saxon England. Malden, MA: Blackwell, 1999.

Blake, E. O. *Liber eliensis*. London: Offices of the Royal Historical Society, 1962.

Boenig, Robert, trans. *Anglo-Saxon Spirituality: Selected Writings*. Mahwah, NJ: Paulist Press, 2001.

Bosworth, Joseph. *An Anglo-Saxon Dictionary: Based on the Manuscript Collections of the Late Joseph Bosworth*. Edited by Thomas Northcote Toller. Oxford: Clarendon Press, 1898.

Fisher, D. J. V. "The Anti-Monastic Reaction in the Reign of Edward the Martyr." *The Cambridge Historical Journal* 10, no. 3 (1952): 254–70.

Foote, Sarah. *Monastic Life in Anglo-Saxon England, c. 600–900*. Cambridge: Cambridge University Press, 2009.

Gneuss, Helmut. "The Origin of Standard Old English and Æthelwold's School at Winchester." *Anglo-Saxon England* 1 (1972): 63–83.

Gretsch, Mechtild. "Æthelwold's Translation of the *Regula Sancti Benedicti* and its Latin Exemplar." Translated by Mechtild Gretsch. *Anglo-Saxon England* 3 (1974): 125–51.

———. "The Benedictine Rule in Old English: A Document of Bishop Æthelwold's Reform Politics." In *Words, Texts, and Manuscripts: Studies in Anglo-Saxon Culture Presented to Helmut Gneuss on the Occasion of his Sixty-Fifth Birthday*, Edited by Michael Korhammer. Cambridge: D. S. Brewer, 1992. 131–58.

———. *Die Regula Sancti Benedicti in England und ihre altenglische Übersetzung*. Munich: Wilhelm Fink Verlag, 1973.

———. *The Intellectual Foundations of the English Benedictine Reform*. Cambridge: Cambridge UP, 1999.

———. "Winchester Vocabulary and Standard Old English: The Vernacular in Late Anglo-Saxon England." *Bulletin of the John Rylands Library* 83, no. 1 (2001): 41–87.

Harper, John. *The Forms and Orders of the Western Liturgy from the Tenth to the Eighteenth Century*. Oxford: Clarendon Press, 1991.

Hofstetter, Walter. "Winchester and the Standardization of Old English Vocabulary." *Anglo-Saxon England* 17 (1988): 139–68.

Hudson, Alison. "From Medieval Saint to Modern Bête Noire: The Case of the *Vitae Æthelwoldi*." *Postmedieval* 4 (2013): 284–95.

Jayatilaka, Rohini. "The Old English Benedictine Rule: Writing for Women and Men." *Anglo-Saxon England* 32 (2003): 147–87.

John, Eric. "The King and the Monks in the Tenth-Century Reformation." In *Orbis Britanniae and Other Studies*. Leicester: Leicester University Press, 1966. 154–80.

Jones, Christopher A. "Ælfric and the Limits of Reform." In *A Companion to Ælfric*, edited by Mary Swan and Hugh Magennis. Leiden: Brill, 2009. 67–108.

Knowles, David. *The Monastic Order in England: A History of its Development from the Times of St. Dunstan to the Fourth Lateran Council, 940–1216.* 2nd ed. Cambridge: Cambridge University Press, 1963.

Niles, John D. *The Idea of Anglo-Saxon England 1066–1901: Remembering, Forgetting, Deciphering, and Renewing the Past.* Malden, MA: Wiley Blackwell, 2015.

O'Brien O'Keeffe, Katherine. *Stealing Obedience: Narratives of Agency and Identity in Later Anglo-Saxon England.* Toronto: University of Toronto Press, 2012.

Oetgen, Jerome. "The Old English Rule of St. Benedict." *The American Benedictine Review* 26 (1975): 38–53.

Parsons, David, ed. *Tenth-century Studies: Essays in Commemoration of the Millennium of the Council of Winchester and the 'Regularis Concordia.'* London: Phillimore, 1975.

Pfaff, Richard W. *The Liturgical Books of Anglo-Saxon England.* Kalamazoo, MI: Medieval Institute Publications, 1995.

———. *The Liturgy in Medieval England: A History.* Cambridge: Cambridge University Press, 2009.

Pratt, David. "The Voice of the King in 'King Edgar's Establishment of Monasteries.'" *Anglo-Saxon England* 41 (2012): 145–204.

Rabin, Andrew. "Holy Bodies, Legal Matters: Reaction and Reform in Ælfric's Eugenia and the Ely Privilege." *Studies in Philology* 110, no. 2 (2013): 220–65.

Smith, Julie. "'I Consider Translation Very Rational': A Vernacular Translation of the Benedictine Rule in the Tenth-Century English Reforms." *American Benedictine Review* 67, no. 1 (2016): 58–80.

Tolhurst, J. B. L., ed. *Introduction to the English Monastic Breviaries.* 1942; Woodbridge: Boydell Press, 1993.

Ward, Benedicta, trans. *Christ Within Me: Prayers and Meditations from the Anglo-Saxon Tradition.* Kalamazoo, MI: Cistercian Publications, 2008.

Werminghoff, Albert. *Concilia aeui Karolini I. Monumenta Germaniae Historica.* Legem Sectio III Concilia 39B. Hannover: Impensis Bibliafolii Hahniani, 1906. 421–56.

Whitelock, Dorothy. "An Account of King Edgar's Establishment of Monasteries." In *Councils and Synods with other Documents Relating to the English Church: I, A.D. 871–1204.* Edited by Dorothy Whitelock. Oxford: Clarendon Press, 1981. 142–54.

———. "The Authorship of the Account of King Edgar's Establishment of the Monasteries." In *Philological Essays: Studies in Old and Middle English Language and Literature in Honour of Herbert Dean Meritt,* edited by James L. Rosier. The Hague: Mouton, 1970. 125–36.

Scriptural Index

Biblical passages are cited according to their locations in Æthelwold's Old English text of the Rule of Saint Benedict by Prologue (Prol.)/ chapter and verse or in Appendices (App) 1, 3, 4. Bracketed chapter and verse numbers indicate location in the Hebrew Bible.

187

50 [51]:17	XXXVIII.3		23:14	II.29
56	XIII.5		27:21	I.6
63	XIII.6		29:19	II.28
64	XIII.6			
65 [66]:10-11	VII.40		*Isaiah*	
65 [66]:12	VII.41		1:2	II.9
66	XIII.2		12:1-6	XIII.10
69 [70]:2	IX.1, XVII.3, XVIII.1,		38:10-20	XIII.10
	XXXV.17		42:3	LXIV.13
72 [73]:22-23	VII.50		58:9	Prol. 18
75	XIII.8			
75 [76]:11	VII.17		*Ezekiel*	
85 [86]:17	XXXV.16		20:27	II.9
87	XIII.7		33:11	Prol. 38
87 [88]:16	VII.53		34:3-4	XXVII.7
89	XIII.7			
91	XIII.8		*Daniel*	
93 [94]:11	VII.15		3:52	XXXV.16
94 [95]:1	IX.3		13:44-62	LXIII.6
94 [95]:8	Prol. 10		14:32-38	App 4
105 [106]:1	VII.46			
113:9 [115:1]	Prol. 30		*Habakkuk*	
117 [118]:1	VII.46		3:1-19	XIII.10
118 [119]:62	XVI.4, XVI.5			
118 [119]:71	VII.54		*Tobias*	
118 [119]:73	VII.54		4:16	IV.9, LXI.14, LXX.7
118 [119]:107	VII.66			
118 [119]:116	LVIII.21		*Sirach*	
118 [119]:164	XVI.1, XVI.3, XVI.5		18:17	XXXI.14
130 [131]:1	VII.3		18:30	VII.19, VII.25
130 [131]:2	VII.4		19:2	XL.7
136 [137]:9	Prol. 28		32:24	III.13
137 [138]:1	XIX.5			
138 [139]:3	VII.16		*Matthew*	
139 [140]:12	VII.58		5:10	IV.33
142	XIII.9		5:39-41	VII.42
			5:44	IV.31
			6:3	II.35
Proverbs			6:10	VII.20
10:19	VI.4, VII.57		6:12	XIII.13
15:3	VII.26, XIX.1		7:3	II.15
16:25	VII.21		7:12	IV.9
18:21	VI.5		7:13-14	Prol. 49